LEAVE NO ONE BEHIND

LEAVE
NO ONE
BEHIND

Hurricane Katrina and the
Rescue of Tulane Hospital

By BILL CAREY

Printed in the United States of America

Library of Congress Control Number: 2006906100

ISBN-13: 978-0-9725680-3-6
ISBN-10: 0-9725680-3-4

Book design by: One Woman Show Design

P.O. Box 58063
Nashville, Tennessee 37205
www.clearbrookpress.com

Contents

REFERENCE GUIDE TO PEOPLE MENTIONED IN THE BOOK

Note: Several physicians listed here practiced at both Tulane and Charity hospitals, and many also work as part-time professors at the Tulane School of Medicine.

Bill Abington, president of operations for Chicago-based equipment distributor Medline

Dr. Bob Ascuitto, pediatric cardiologist

Tyrone Augusta, director of facility services for DePaul-Tulane Behavioral Health Center

Tim Beasley, EMT supervisor for Medical City Children's Hospital in Dallas

Dr. Robert Beckerman, pediatric pulmonologist

Dr. Ruth Berggren, infectious disease specialist

Dan Bitton, helicopter pilot who normally flies for the Winthrop Harbor (Illinois) Police Department

Kathleen Blanco, Louisiana's governor

Kathy Bobbs, chief executive officer at Women's and Children's Hospital in Lafayette, Louisiana

Leona Boullion, chief nursing officer at Women's and Children's Hospital

Jack Bovender, chairman and chief executive office of Nashville-based HCA, which owns and operates Tulane Hospital

Richard Bracken, HCA's president and chief operating officer

Chuck Brainerd, pilot and the owner of Firehawk Helicopters Inc.

Sonny Breaux, supervisor for Tulane's maintenance department

Warren Breaux, Tulane's deputy chief of police

Byron Brimmer, respiratory therapist at Tulane

Silvio Carrillo, CNN producer

Yonnie Chesley, vice president of human resources at HCA

Stiles Clarke, medical director for LifeNet (a division of Air Methods Corp.)

Tim Coffey, chief operating officer of Chalmette Hospital in New Orleans

David Critchlow, HCA's head of government relations

Dr. Tyler Curiel, hematologist and medical oncologist

Rich Cutillo, operations manager at Louis Armstrong Airport

Dr. Steven Davidoff, resident internal medicinist

Fred Dejean, volunteer from Lafayette, Louisiana

Jayne Dejean, director of nursing resources for Women's and Children's Hospital

Dr. Ben duBoisblanc, director of Charity Hospital's intensive care unit

Andre DuPlessis, chief operating officer at Lakeside Hospital in Metairie, Louisiana

Rochelle Dugas, legislative director for Louisiana Governor Kathleen Blanco

Dr. Melanie Ehrlich, professor of biochemistry and genetics at Tulane School of Medicine

Alan Fabian, chief operating officer at Southwest Medical Center

Heather Fallon, mother of a Tulane pediatric patient

Dr. Leron Finger, pediatric critical care physician

Gene Floyd, amateur radio operator

Cheryl Friday, neonatal intensive care nurse at Woman's and Children's Hospital

Timothy Gabriel, Tulane patient

Dr. Bill Gill, neonatologist and Tulane's chief of medical staff

Elaine Gimlin, director of supply for West Florida Regional Hospital

Jeff Goldblatt, Fox News Channel reporter

Kim Graham, Tulane's director of pediatric services

Dawn Guidry, Tulane's food services director

Sanjay Gupta, CNN reporter

Chuck Hall, head of HCA's North Florida division

Dr. Lee Hamm, internal medicinist and nephrologist

Sam Hazen, chief executive officer of HCA's western group of hospitals

Michael Hedges, *Houston Chronicle* reporter

Rob Heifner, Tulane vice president

John Holland, pilot with LifeNet (a division of Air Methods Corp.)

Jeanne James, Tulane's chief medical officer

George Jamison, Tulane's director of facility services

Colby Johnson, respiratory therapist at Women's and Children's Hospital

Ed Jones, head of supply for HCA's Eastern group of hospitals

Dr. Mike Kiernan, pediatric pulmonologist

Dr. Ross Klingsberg, internal medicinist

Sergeant Kraft (first name unknown), U.S. Marine

Mel Lagarde, head of HCA's Delta division of hospitals, and the senior HCA person at Tulane during Hurricane Katrina

Dr. Joe Lasky, pulmonary critical care specialist

Max Lauderdale, chief executive officer of Lakeview Regional Medical Center in Covington, Louisiana

Bob Loup, operations supervisor at the Louis Armstrong Airport

Dr. Jennifer McGee, resident surgeon

Dr. Norm McSwain, surgeon and head of trauma at Charity Hospital

Greg Miller, pilot with St. Louis Helicopter LLC

Jim Montgomery, Tulane's chief executive officer

Howard Myers, truck driver for Exum Energy Inc.

Dr. Jeff Myers, surgeon

Ray Nagin, mayor of New Orleans

Jennifer Neely, community relations coordinator with HCA

Evelyn Nolting, director of clinical services for DePaul-Tulane Behavioral Health Center

Robin Norwood, mother of a Tulane pediatric patient

Sharif Omar, associate vice president at Tulane

Randy Pierce, emergency radio communications coordinator for the state of Florida

Marcus Reinders, manager at the W New Orleans hotel

Christina Riviere, pediatric nurse at Tulane

Sue Roesky, mother of a Tulane pediatric patient

Dr. Nancy Ross-Ascuitto, pediatric cardiologist

Dr. Marta Rozans, pediatric hematologist and oncologist

Micky Rozans, son of Dr. Marta Rozans

Sam Rozans, son of Dr. Marta Rozans

Kim Ryan, Tulane's chief operating officer

Susan Sanborn, student nurse at Charity Hospital

Steve Schaaf, father of a Tulane neonatal patient

Bill Schmitt, amateur radio operator

Francesco Simeone, intensive care specialist

Brad Smith, father of a Tulane patient

David Smith, director of contracting for HCA's north Florida division

Mike Sonnier, air services coordinator for Acadian Ambulance Service Inc.

Deborah Spell, chief nursing officer at Southwest Medical Center

Ritchie Stanley, Louisiana state trooper

Carla Staxrud, EMT with Guardian Emergency Medical Services

Tia Styles, mother of a Tulane pediatric patient

Danita Sullivan, Tulane's chief nursing officer

Peggy Taylor, abdominal transplant patient at Tulane

Dwayne Thomas, chief executive officer of Charity and University hospitals

Theo Titus, amateur radio operator

Karen Troyer-Caraway, Tulane vice president

Jeff Tully, Tulane vice president

Cheryl Turano, volunteer and daughter of Tulane COO Kim Ryan

Adora Udoji, CNN reporter

Marie Patty Walker, manager of Joe Patti's Seafood in Pensacola, Florida

Brian Weldy, head of HCA's design and construction division

David Whalen, chief executive officer of Twin Cities Hospital in Niceville, Florida

Jill Williams, mother of a Tulane neonatal patient

Roy Williams, aviation director at Louis Armstrong Airport

Donna Yurdin, human resources executive with HCA

Introduction

T his book is dedicated with gratitude to all the employees, physicians, volunteers, and friends who are part of the expansive
group we call The HCA Family. While the story contained in
these pages affected the nation in a profound way, and is therefore one I
hope everyone will read and appreciate, it is for you, The HCA Family,
that it was written.

The one constant I've been privileged to observe throughout my
forty-two years in health care is the incredible commitment, dedication,
and self-sacrifice of the doctors, nurses, and other health professionals who
staff this nation's hospitals. On countless occasions I have watched them
perform the most remarkable feats of service for their fellow human
beings, in many cases without concern for their own health or safety.

Never was this culture of personal commitment and responsibility
more clearly manifested than during the evacuation of HCA's Tulane
Hospital following the New Orleans flooding caused by Hurricane
Katrina. This book tells the story of that culture and of the men and
women who, throughout the week of that disaster, toiled at grueling tasks

in the most wretched conditions imaginable, with the single-minded purpose of saving their patients and their colleagues. In the finest traditions of those past and present health care professionals, they did what had to be done and never gave up. In the end, they rescued more than 1,200 patients, colleagues, and family members.

This book, then, is also a tribute to all those throughout HCA who directly or indirectly gave so much to the saving of countless lives in New Orleans. In a much larger sense, it is a tribute to all those across the country who, every day, in every hospital, heal the sick and injured and care for the dying with love and compassion.

Jack O. Bovender
Chairman and CEO
Hospital Corporation of America

Chapter One
Touring Downtown

T he rain came, the wind came, and the surge came. They shook the walls of the seven-story building and kept most of its more than one thousand inhabitants awake that night. The storm wasn't steady; it came in strong bursts you could hear from inside the building if you stopped what you were doing or what you were saying and listened for it. And if you put your hand on an exterior wall, you might have felt a slight vibration. Of course, you could also see the ferocity of Hurricane Katrina from inside Tulane University Hospital and Clinic; that is, if you were brave enough to get near a window.

It was an exciting night. At about nine p.m. a CNN crew including reporter Adora Udoji and producer Silvio Carrillo showed up. A hospital official gave them a tour of the hospital, showing them some of the things the staff had done in advance of the storm. The national news network showed Tulane personnel making last-minute preparations for what appeared to be the biggest hurricane ever to hit New Orleans; taking care of fifty-eight patients that the government had unexpectedly transported to Tulane from the Superdome the night before; moving the hospital's emergency room and pharmacy away from the ground floor; and serving hot food to everyone in the building as if nothing was amiss. When the storm hit, the journalists asked permission to stay (it did, after all, seem like the safest place in the city). For the rest of the night the network broadcast sound bites from Tulane people such as physician Mike Kiernan, chief medical officer Jeanne James, and chief operating officer Kim Ryan. It was, for all involved, a bit heady.

The Tulane staff got along fine with the CNN people – except for the time the visitors tried to step outside in the middle of the storm. "I've been through many hurricanes before, and I didn't really fear it, so I thought we'd step outside and get a live shot of the storm blowing things around," said Carrillo. "We tried for a few minutes, but they finally told us it was too dangerous and that we should go back inside." The language may, in fact, have been harsher than Carrillo remembered. "I told them to get their asses back inside," George Jamison, Tulane's head of plant operations, recalled months later. "We had enough things to worry about without them getting hurt by flying debris, and I didn't want the front door opening and closing."

Local television and radio stations went down, as did the city's power grid. One physician later recalled that about four a.m. he "heard a loud explosion and the lights went out for a second, and then I looked out and saw a transformer blowing up just down the street." But this didn't take anyone by surprise. As soon as electricity went out, the hospital's emergency generators came to life, providing complete power to the red outlets and partial power to the air conditioner.

The frame of Tulane's main building held up fine during the hurricane. But the torrent of rain and wind was too much for some of the windows in the thirty-year-old structure. During the course of the storm, many leaked water. And there were a couple of places where window frames became separated from the building itself. This became such a concern in one part of the hospital that the abdominal transplant patients were moved out of their rooms. "For a while I remember watching the wind out my window, and it really didn't scare me that much," said Peggy Taylor, a patient who had undergone a liver transplant a few days earlier. "But when it got really bad they moved us out into the hallway."

So the storm itself was an adventure. It gave the inhabitants of Tulane Hospital a concern or two, and it worried their friends and family members, who were glued to their televisions all night. It also did considerable damage to some nearby buildings, many of which were affiliated with the hospital. Bob Ascuitto was a pediatric cardiologist who practiced at Tulane Hospital and taught at the adjacent Tulane Medical School. Like many professors, Dr. Ascuitto decided to sit out the storm in his office. When Katrina hit, he was terrified. "The hurricane struck with a fury," he later wrote in an article for a professional publication called *Congenital Cardiology Today.*

> I was resting in a small office connected to our laboratory, when suddenly I was startled by a rumbling and shrieking sound.
>
> As I cautiously opened the door to the main laboratory [which had an exterior window], it suddenly was torn from my hand. Papers, books, surgical instruments, and various types of equipment were flying around the room, ultimately being sucked out through broken windows. A fifty-pound roller pump disappeared into the darkness. It was as if a black hole had stationed itself outside the medical center.
>
> I clung to a sink to avoid being pulled into the whirling debris . . . Several of my colleagues rushed to my aid, and collectively we managed to escape safely. Hyperventilating, my heart pounding, and drenched with cold sweat, I dashed through darkened hallways and an enclosed bridge to the Hospital, to help with patients. As I crossed the bridge, the rain obscured most of

the medical center; however, I did witness a palm tree flying through the air like a misguided arrow.

By the latter part of the morning of Monday, August 29, 2005, Hurricane Katrina had abated. By noon it stopped raining altogether, and the sun came out. The CNN crew left, in search of more compelling footage of storm damage and suffering people than they could find at or near Tulane. By the middle of the afternoon some people staying at the hospital ventured outside to see how the rest of downtown had fared. "Several of us walked up and down Canal Street and Tulane Avenue and congratulated ourselves for surviving," said Kim Ryan, Tulane's chief operating officer. "The 'big one' had come and gone and didn't do what they said it was going to do. There was tons of wind damage at the Hyatt [Regency Hotel] and many palm trees had come down, but that was pretty much it."

Marta Rozans, a pediatric hematologist and oncologist at Tulane, was on duty at the hospital, where her two sons (ages fourteen and eleven) were also riding out the storm. On Monday afternoon, they walked outside and had a good time. "People kind of felt like saying to the sky, 'Is that the worst you can do?'" she later said.

With the storm over, people began trying to telephone family members elsewhere in the country – not easy considering most cellular phone systems weren't working. Peoples' concern shifted from their own safety and well-being to the condition of their homes. The maintenance staff began to assess damage to the several structures that comprised the Tulane Hospital campus. Senior doctors began preparing their junior counterparts and residents for what to expect once the city returned to life. "The head of trauma surgery advised us that trauma and violence would spike in eighteen hours and then medical disease would sharply increase thirty-six hours later," recalled Steven Davidoff, a resident physician who wrote a lengthy account of his experiences a few weeks later. "This would include heart attacks, strokes, and seizures as patients ran out of their medications."

There was a lot of work to do, and important things to get ready for – but certainly the type of thing a hospital is prepared to deal with in such a situation. And, although no one had any idea when normal power would be restored to the city, Tulane had multiple levels of emergency electricity, all of which appeared to be working reliably. The hospital had enough diesel fuel to last another two days or so, and its parent company was already making plans to send in another truckload as soon as the roads were clear.

Late Monday afternoon the staff at Tulane Hospital began moving the facility's emergency room, pharmacy, and food service back to the ground floor of the hospital, where all three had been before being moved upstairs in advance of the storm. As the sun set that evening, some people began making the assumption they would be returning to their homes, and turning over to the next shift, on Tuesday. Top hospital officials even lay down to get some sleep that night.

All in all, people generally thought, Hurricane Katrina was overrated as far as natural disasters were concerned.

But on Monday night – accounts vary as to the time – something peculiar began to happen. In spite of the fact that the rain had stopped, water began accumulating in the streets. By eight p.m., water in front of the hospital's main entrance reached ankle depth; a few hours later it was twice that. By the time it got dark, emergency military vehicles driving along Canal Street were leaving behind a wake that pushed water into Tulane's lobby and emergency room, making it hazardous to walk on the slippery tile floor. Plant operations then posted someone to monitor the water level and keep an eye on the emergency power generator in the basement. Thirty minutes later he came back with news that the water was rising an inch every five minutes, and that it would soon render the emergency power system inoperative.

No one could explain why it was happening. But one thing was certain: the city of New Orleans was flooding.

Chapter Two
Stockpiling Kitty Litter

By the time Hurricane Katrina hit the southern coast of Louisiana, the company that owned and operated Tulane Hospital had been preparing for the disaster for two days. Actually – to be more accurate – HCA had been preparing long before that.

HCA was originally founded in 1968 under the name Hospital Corporation of America. Among its founders were Jack Massey, then the chairman of Kentucky Fried Chicken; Thomas Frist Sr., a cardiologist whose son, Bill Frist, would later become U.S. Senate majority leader; and Thomas Frist Jr., who would be the company's CEO through much of the 1980s and 1990s. Contrary to popular opinion, the Nashville-based firm wasn't the first for-profit hospital company in America. But because of its founders' salesmanship and ability to secure financing, it has always been the largest. At its peak in the mid-1990s, HCA owned more than four hundred hospitals. At the time of Hurricane Katrina it owned about half that number, many of them along the Gulf Coast or southern Atlantic Coast – in hurricane-prone cities such as Houston,

Texas; Lafayette, Louisiana; Gulfport, Mississippi; and Palm Beach, Florida.

Prior to Katrina everyone at HCA regarded 2004 to have been the "Year of the Hurricane." That, after all, was the year Florida was hit by one storm after another. Knowing that many of the lessons learned from that year would prove valuable, HCA organized a debriefing in Orlando to review what had worked and what had not. One of the practices to come out of the January 2005 session, for instance, was for the company to pre-position supplies such as back-up generators and diesel fuel close, but not too close, to hospitals in the impact zone. Another lesson was to assume in a disaster situation that help from outside authorities would not arrive in time. Be grateful if it comes; but assume it won't.

Like many of HCA's hospitals, Tulane University Hospital and Clinic had a unique story. The Tulane University School of Medicine traced its origins to 1834, when seven New Orleans doctors organized the Medical College of Louisiana. That institution later became part of the University of Louisiana, which subsequently became Tulane University. For nearly a century Tulane Medical School did not attach its name to a hospital; its students trained and practiced at other New Orleans hospitals. That situation changed in 1976, when Tulane's three-hundred-bed teaching hospital and ambulatory clinic opened.

From the beginning, the board of Tulane Medical School looked for creative ways to operate its hospital. In its early years it took the bold step of "farming out" its operations to a Nashville-based hospital management firm called Hospital Affiliates International (a company started in hopes of repeating HCA's success). In 1995 Tulane went a step further, selling 80 percent of its ownership to Hospital Corporation of America successor Columbia/HCA Healthcare Corp. (which later became known as, simply, HCA). Under this arrangement, HCA owned and operated the facility in a partnership with Tulane University.

So hurricanes weren't new to HCA, and they weren't new to New

Orleans (which experienced 125 mile per hour winds when Hurricane Betsy struck in 1965). At the beginning of the 2005 storm season hospital administrators at Tulane told their department heads to see that all the usual procedures were followed. The hospital was stocked with extra food and water. Every department of the hospital was supplied with flashlights and batteries. Three extra pallets of rags and sheets were brought in. The hospital was outfitted with hurricane shutters to protect many of its ground-floor windows. The plant operations department checked to make certain the hospital had an ample supply of kitty litter – fifteen hundred pounds of it, to be exact.

The stockpile of kitty litter might have seemed odd at the time. It certainly wouldn't seem odd during the Katrina flood, when the hospital lost running water (and with it, the ability to flush toilets). Asked after the storm about his department's stash of kitty litter, Tulane's head of plant operations George Jamison said it was one of many small things that differentiated his facility from others. "We ain't like any other hospital," said Jamison, a former Coast Guard senior chief who had a nautical-style window carved out of his door in the basement of Tulane Hospital. "As far as I'm concerned, there ain't no hospital like it in HCA or anywhere else. We have everything for an emergency around here.

"What do you think we were doing with fifteen hundred pounds of kitty litter? Because we knew that someday we might have to use the bathroom without running water, that's why!"

Since natural disasters frequently knock out electrical systems, some of the most important preparations had to do with the hospital's power supply. Tulane, like most hospitals, had a diesel-powered emergency backup generator fixed to the building for times when Entergy, the utility providing power to the city of New Orleans, went down. To be more specific, the hospital had five such generators – three supplying power to its newer building and two supplying power to the old. These backup generators provided AC power to a separate system of red electrical outlets located throughout the facility.

Unfortunately, those backup generators were on the ground floor – this in a city located below sea level and adjacent to two large bodies of water.

In the days before Hurricane Katrina, HCA's design and construction division had a fifteen-hundred-kilowatt generator (so large it sat on the bed of a tractor trailer) sent to the New Orleans hospital. "The normal emergency power systems can't operate the air conditioner at full capacity by themselves," said Brian Weldy, head of HCA's design and construction division. "So we mainly rent those tractor-trailer generators as a supplement to a hospital's normal emergency power system. But if the emergency power system goes out, then the tractor-trailer generators can be a backup to the normal emergency power system." To fuel the backup generators, HCA had about five hundred pounds of diesel fuel sent to Tulane (as it did to the company's other hospitals in the path of the hurricane). The company stationed a much larger fuel supply at the HCA-owned Lakeview Regional Medical Center in Covington that could be shuttled to Tulane after the storm came through.

Since the electrical components of the tractor-trailer generator sat about six feet above the ground, Tulane figured the "generator on wheels" could sustain a certain amount of flooding. The only backups after that were three portable gas generators, which had a very limited capacity.

Personnel preparations are at least as important as stockpiling supplies. In advance of hurricanes, HCA hospitals tell each department to carefully plan which people will be on duty when foreseeable natural disasters strike. People assigned to the so-called "A Teams" are told when they come in for such situations to bring bedding, extra food, and toiletries. They are also told to make preparations to remain at the hospital through the duration of the disaster – so they need to arrange for the care of their wives, husbands, children, parents, and pets in advance.

This was easier said than done. Ideally, HCA (as would any employer) would have preferred its employees to evacuate their families to a safe place in advance of a hurricane. But that wasn't possible for many people. Some were single parents. Some had relatives who couldn't be moved. Some couldn't afford to evacuate their families. "The truth of the matter is that many people who work in some of the jobs here live from payday to payday and have done so for five generations, and some of them have never even owned an automobile," said Jamison. "Some of the ones that do own an automobile can't afford to just drive to Jackson, Mississippi, and stay at a Holiday Inn for five days."

There were also some people who worked at Tulane Hospital whose spouses also had to work through the hurricane. Marta Rozans was a Tulane doctor, the wife of a doctor at the New Orleans VA Hospital, and the mother of two boys. As a matter of routine, whenever there was a hurricane coming and she was on duty, she and her sons packed up their necessities and came to Tulane Hospital with plans to stay in the building through the entire experience. "I wanted my kids there with me because there was no other place for them to be," she said. "And to be honest, there was no one else for me to send them to in such a situation."

Over the years Tulane's hurricane experiences had led to some family members having regular duties. Cheryl Turano, the twenty-four-year-old daughter of Tulane COO Kim Ryan, came in that Sunday with the assumption that she'd be doing the same thing she had done in previous storms. "Usually, I'm the one who opens a day care for the children of staff members," said Turano, a pre-K schoolteacher. In an attempt to encourage staff members to evacuate their children, the hospital's administration decided not to open a day care center on the eve of Katrina. However, Turano would later be put to work on more formidable tasks.

Then there were the patient preparations. In the days before Katrina doctors worked hard to discharge as many of the sick and injured as possible. "I spoke briefly with each patient and warned them of the monstrous storm destined to hit us within twenty-four hours," Davidoff later wrote, in an experience indicative of those of other doctors.

> I asked each patient if they were prepared to stay in the hospital for what I expected to be two or three days without power, or if there was any chance they could go home and prepare. Through this process I was able to convince two additional patients to be discharged.
>
> We spent the next several hours frantically working on preparing the discharge paperwork. What generally would take twenty minutes took forty, because everything seemed to be moving so much slower that day. Later that day, I spent about thirty to forty minutes with each patient and their family. I wanted them to know (if they didn't already know) what was going to happen. I reassured them that we would continue to provide them food, water, and the medical service they required.

By Saturday the patient count was down to 120 – a low number considering the hospital's usual population at that time of year. But most of the patients had with them family members. Added to that amount were a large number of medical students or Tulane professors who decided to "sit out" the storm at or near their offices (in buildings adjacent to Tulane Hospital). So, by Sunday evening, there were more than a thousand people in Tulane Hospital and the adjacent medical school buildings.

As for the hospital administration, HCA made it a regular practice for the top executives at the hospital to come to the facility and remain there throughout natural disasters, establishing a so-called "command center" in a central location at the hospital. (This military vernacular might have seemed unusual in advance of the storm, but appropriate in the days after it.) Normally this arrangement would make the hospital CEO head of the command center. But Mel Lagarde, head of HCA's Delta division of hospitals, chose to sit out Hurricane Katrina at Tulane. "It is standard procedure for me to go base my command at one of the hospitals, and I had done it many times before at Tulane," he said.

Once the "command center" was established, it became the heart of the hospital in much the same way Combat Information Center became the heart of a navy ship in wartime. All phone calls were routed into the command center; all department heads reported to the command center; and the place was staffed twenty-four hours a day. Tulane's command center – headed by (in order) Lagarde, Tulane CEO Jim Montgomery, and Tulane COO Kim Ryan – was "established" on Saturday afternoon. Among the other people in the command center were Jeff Tully (vice president); Rob Heifner (vice president); Danita Sullivan (chief nursing officer); Jeanne James (chief medical officer); and Mike Kiernan, a pediatric pulmonologist who volunteered to help during the storm.

Under normal conditions Tulane's security officers are armed with forty-caliber pistols, carried in a discreet manner. As the hurricane bore down on New Orleans, security guards broke out their more visible weaponry, including semi-automatic rifles and shotguns. A staff of twenty-nine during the storm, they made preparations to guard all six structures in the Tulane Medical Center complex. "We've been through storms before," said deputy chief of police Warren Breaux. "You hope for the best and prepare for the worst. And one of those very bad scenarios we prepare for is the hospital being rushed by thousands of people from all over the city."

The exodus from the city of New Orleans that Sunday may have been the greatest single evacuation in American history; the South certainly hadn't seen anything quite like it since the Civil

War. The governor of Louisiana and the mayor of New Orleans told everyone who possibly could leave to do so, and police fanned out across the city to execute the order. Both sides of Interstate 10, the main route leading northwest to Baton Rouge, were made northbound. Hotels as distant as Atlanta overflowed with hurricane evacuees. At the urging of New Orleans Mayor Ray Nagin, people who stayed in the city were told to come to the Superdome during the storm rather than remain in their homes.

The staff at Tulane stayed busy that day. Doctors made lists of their patients, their conditions, and their electrical needs. The maintenance staff did last-minute checks to make sure the backup generators were working, made certain there was no loose debris of any kind outside the hospital, and nailed plywood shutters to many of the ground floor windows. Every set of blinds in the building was lowered, and (to the degree possible) patients were moved away from windows. With hundreds of people in the building in need of a place to stay, several people in the command center got to work finding places for everyone to sleep. "We did a top to bottom walk-through of the facility to find every bed, mattress, gurney, and reclining chair," vice president of business development Karen Troyer-Caraway said later. "Then we set up a spreadsheet to try to assign beds to people." Among the people who pitched in was fourteen-year-old Sam Rozans. "I moved quite a few of those mattresses," he said.

As staff and family members were assigned a place to sleep, they were also given meal tickets and green wristbands (green being the school color of Tulane). "When we were first given the wristbands, we were joking about the idea that they were giving them to us so they could sort out our bodies when they found us all dead after the hurricane," one employee said later. But those bands turned out to be extremely important later in the week, when Tulane staffers would be evacuated to an airport crawling with evacuees from all over the New Orleans area.

In spite of the staff's efforts to tabulate a head count, many of the people who came to Tulane on Sunday to weather the storm did so without telling anyone in charge. The medical complex consisted of six large buildings: the main hospital, Tulane Medical School Building, the twenty-four story Tidewater Building, the Deming Pavilion, the J. Bennett Johnston Building, and the Elks Place Building. Many of the physicians, medical students, and other people with offices in the complex came in on Sunday with (by their estimate) ample supplies to take care of themselves through the storm. On Monday and Tuesday all of these people would migrate to the hospital building needing food, water, and – most importantly – a way out. The number of people Tulane didn't know about on Sunday, but for whom Tulane would be responsible for later that week, is one of the reasons the hospital never had an accurate head count of how many people took part in the airlift.

To further complicate the situation, not everyone associated with Tulane made plans to stay in one of the hospital buildings. Officials at the hospital made arrangements for family members of staff to stay at the Park Plaza Hotel (two blocks away) for a discount. "We told staff that if their family members wanted this reduced rate, they had to come by the command center on Sunday and get a sheet of paper with our letterhead on it, which would identify them to the hotel," said Jeff Tully. Tully estimated that two hundred rooms were rented through this process, although he had no idea how many people were staying in those rooms. "For all I know there might have been six to a room."

Although Tulane made preparations to feed and shelter all of its patients, staff, and family members, the hospital encouraged everyone to bring extra supplies. Interviewed months later, one physician said his "survival pack" included, among other things, three flashlights, batteries, candles, fruit, bread, power bars, cold cuts, cookies, water, juice, and a bottle of wine. People brought so many supplies, in fact, that relatively few people ate at the hospital's cafeteria on Sunday night.

On Sunday, with the National Weather Service predicting heavy flooding from the storm surge, people began moving the emergency room from the ground floor to the endoscopy suite on the third floor. This section of the hospital was chosen because it had an adequate number of red electrical outlets, which work when a hospital goes to backup emergency power. Other people were involved in moving the pharmacy from the ground floor to the fourth floor, and the food service from the ground floor to the fifth floor. "The elevators were very crowded that day," one staffer later said.

New Orleans had been hit by hurricanes before, but at the last minute many of those storms veered away or downgraded to considerably less than their original strength. No doubt, many of the people who were staying at Tulane Hospital believed something similar might happen again. But as Sunday afternoon became Sunday evening, and the streets of New Orleans became quiet, that's not what the National Weather Service was saying.

Here, in fact, are excerpts from the official forecast and hurricane warning issued to New Orleans late Sunday morning:

> Most of the area will be uninhabitable for weeks . . . perhaps longer. At least one-half of well-constructed homes will have roof and wall failure. All gabled roofs will fail . . . leaving those homes severely damaged or destroyed.
>
> High-rise office and apartment buildings will sway dangerously . . . a few to the point of total collapse. All windows will blow out.
>
> Airborne debris will be widespread, and may include heavy items such as household appliances and even light vehicles. Sport utility vehicles and light trucks will be moved. The blown debris will create additional destruction. Persons, pets, and livestock exposed to the winds will face certain death if struck.

Power outages will last for weeks, as most power poles will be down and transformers destroyed. Water shortages will make human suffering incredible by modern standards.

Danita Sullivan, Tulane's chief nursing officer and a lifelong Louisiana resident, said later she would never forget what it was like to read the forecast. "I quietly looked at it. Then I shut my door and called my sister and said, 'OK, just in case something happens, I love you.' She asked me if I was scared. And I said, 'I'm not scared that I won't survive. I am scared for all these people. We have so many people here, and I'm not sure what will happen to all of them.'"

Sullivan then went and found George Jamison, who, as head of plant operations, seemed the most knowledgeable about the structure of the building. "I asked George if the building would stand," she said. "He looked at me and said, 'Yeah, it'll stand. We'll be all right,' and he had no question in his voice. I don't know if he was lying or not but that was all I needed to hear."

As the sun went down Sunday night, everyone seemed to be dealing differently with the personal stress caused by the incoming storm. "Some people were worried, some were tending to their children, others were watching DVDs, and some pretended that nothing was going to happen," Davidoff wrote.

By the time the first signs of the storm appeared outside, everyone seemed to be ready and braced for it. But there was one notable exception. Twenty-six-year-old Sharif Omar was associate vice-president of operations for Tulane Hospital. While his colleagues were making preparations for the storm, he was in Houston attending his own bachelor party. "When I left New Orleans for the weekend it was a Category Two storm headed for the Florida Gulf Coast, but obviously that changed as the weekend went on," he said. "That weekend, I think I spent more time on the phone than I did partying." Sharif's superiors at Tulane told him not to come back. But, sensing he was needed more than anyone would admit, he decided to return. Sunday, he headed south toward New Orleans, going, in his own words, "a hundred miles per hour into the city while everyone else was going out of the city at two miles an hour." Since all four lanes of Interstate 10 were northbound that day, Omar drove Highway 61, known to locals as the Airline Highway. "There was a policeman at every turnpike," he later said. "None of them knew what to make of me."

Sharif went by his apartment and packed a quick bag, then got to the hospital at 5:30 p.m. "The big gusts and the heavy rains had begun," he said.

Katrina had arrived.

That night, as rain deluged New Orleans, there were some unexpected setbacks at Tulane. Two of the hospital's top administrators – vice president Jeff Tully and chief medical officer Jeanne James – got sick. "I had just been in Central America, and I must have picked something up there because I got sick as a dog," Tully later said. "I wanted to throw up and I couldn't and finally they just made me go to the emergency room, where they put me on IVs." James, meanwhile, had a bad asthma attack during the hurricane and was unable to move around much because of it.

But the big surprise came from the federal government. On Sunday night representatives of the U.S. Department of Homeland Security (DHS) called Tulane saying it needed buildings in which to stage a so-called Disaster Medical Assistance Team (DMAT). The main purpose of the DMAT unit would be to take care of some of the more medically fragile people who had sought shelter from the hurricane at the Louisiana Superdome a few blocks away. (An estimated twenty thousand people flocked to the dome the night before the storm.) The DHS assured Tulane officials they would provide doctors, nurses, and equipment necessary to operate the DMAT unit. The people and their equipment were in Baton Rouge and would be there by ten p.m, the DHS said. All the DHS needed was a safe, solid building, appropriate for such a function.

A DHS official came and looked over some clinic space at Tulane Hospital, and Tulane officials agreed. "Obviously we had to agree in order to do something for the community," Tulane's Kim Ryan said, "but we also figured it might be useful to have federal government officials in the building with us."

However, things didn't work out exactly the way the DHS said they would. The medically fragile weren't supposed to arrive until about two hours after the DHS official's visit. But twenty minutes after he left, a busload of people showed up from the Superdome. There were fifty-eight of them, plus their accompanying family members. When they first got there, the process of triaging them began. "I watched my mother [Kim Ryan] do it for a minute and then grabbed a clipboard and a sheet of paper and started doing it myself," said Cheryl Turano. "I was told to put down their name, date of birth, and everything they said was wrong with them. I'd write down if they had a heart condition, or diabetes, or asthma, or pain in the legs, or whatever it was."

Steven Davidoff, one of the physicians who triaged the Superdome arrivals, described the process this way: "These were patients who were on the verge of being hospitalized and people who could have been in a nursing home but weren't," wrote Davidoff. "Under normal conditions, treating such patients would have required things such as paperwork, documentation, and proof of insurance. But not this time. Jeanne James, the chief medical officer, told me just to treat them and take care of their pressing needs, and to write down their name, the name of their accompanying people, and the diseases or conditions they had." Davidoff also wrote that his training as a certified wilderness EMT was more valuable to him that week than medical school.

The staff and equipment that were supposed to accompany the DMAT unit didn't arrive that night, or the next night, or any night. In fact, months after the hurricane, no one at Tulane or HCA had ever heard what happened to the DMAT unit that was supposed to come. What did happen was that on the eve of the hurricane, Tulane's effective patient load increased by nearly fifty percent and the hospital's demand for oxygen doubled. For the time being, the "Superdome people" (as they would be referred to for the next several days), were placed in a seventh floor lobby area stocked with extra cots, chairs, pillows, and gurneys. Turano spent the next three days caring for them. "I got to know most of them on a first-name basis," she later said.

Chapter Three
Rising Tide

S ome people at Tulane Hospital actually got a good night's sleep Monday night. They went to bed thinking the storm was gone and everything was getting back to normal, and didn't wake up until the hospital was surrounded by between two and four feet of water. "The first time I heard about the flood was when my phone rang and woke me up," said physician Steven Davidoff. "It was my friend from Chicago, and the first thing he asks me is what floor I'm on. I told him the fourth. I said, 'Why are you asking?' He says, 'Go look out the window!'"

Others were up all night, nervously watching the water rise and wondering what was causing it, what it meant, and what was going to happen because of it. Those who stayed awake were involved in one of many subplots as it became obvious that the flood was real and it wasn't like anything the city of New Orleans had ever seen.

People who were in the hospital that night have different accounts of when things happened – for some reason the timeline is harder to construct that night than any other. What is certain is that on Monday afternoon, from about noon until four p.m., the streets of New Orleans were dry enough to walk around on. Around six hours later, with water apparently rising, the decision was made to move the emergency room back up to the third floor – this only a few hours after it had been moved from the third floor back down to the ground floor.

According to people interviewed for this book, the most maddening thing about Monday night and early Tuesday morning was the lack of information about what was happening. Only twenty-four hours earlier, it had been almost impossible to shut out the detailed, and horrifying, weather forecast predicting what might soon happen in New Orleans. Now, no one at the hospital could get an explanation of what was happening. "After a couple of hours of watching the water rise, we went back to [vice president] Rob Heifner's office where there is this huge map of New Orleans," said Kim Ryan. "We started looking at where the levees were, and we started guessing that one of them had collapsed. But we weren't certain."

Televisions and radios were of little use, as practically all stations in the New Orleans area were shut down in the hours after Katrina (except an AM radio station based in Kenner that some people listened to). People were, however, able to make occasional phone calls to those in other parts of the country who were watching television. News that a levee had possibly broken began to filter in. "I remember that the CNN producer who had been here the night before [Silvio Carrillo] called at some point to tell us there was flooding in the Lower Ninth Ward, but I don't remember exactly when that was," said Karen Troyer-Caraway. Reporters, however, were just as confused as everyone else. "I was over in the Ninth Ward, watching and interviewing refugees who were filtering onto this interstate ramp," Carrillo said. "It was dark, but because of the police lights and the floodlights we could see pretty well. And there was water everywhere, in some cases all the way up to the roofs of houses. But we honestly had no idea what was causing it."

In fact, interviewed months after the event, Carrillo seemed to remember that Troyer-Caraway told him about the flood, not the other way around. "I think I learned about it from Karen to be honest," he said. "Sometime after we got over to the Ninth Ward, maybe at midnight or one a.m. or so, I got a text message from Karen on my cell phone telling me the water was rising at a foot an hour and they were going to evacuate the hospital. So I messaged her back and told her to call my assignment desk in Atlanta. She did that, and, as I understand it, they immediately put her on the air."

News of the flood spread with less speed than might have been expected. Mel Lagarde and Jim Montgomery, the highest-ranking HCA officials in the building, actually went to bed around eleven that night. About an hour later, with flood waters reaching alarming levels, Kim Ryan called the Louisiana Hospital Association. It had no explanation for what was occurring. "I don't remember who we spoke to, but I told her we were in the process of moving our emergency room back downstairs and we were taking on water and we needed to know what was happening," she said. "As I remember it, she put me on hold for a while and then she came back and said she didn't know of any reason why we were seeing what we were seeing. But we were strongly encouraged to move our ER back upstairs. That was when I woke up Jim [Montgomery] and Mel [Lagarde]."

It was at this point, with water inexplicably rising, that morale hit the low point for many people at Tulane Hospital. They had already been through what they thought was the brunt of the storm, and had been under the impression that the great Hurricane Katrina adventure was winding down. Now, water was rising, no one could explain why, and no one was sure how high it would rise. "For all we knew, the water was going to rise to fifteen feet all across New Orleans," Montgomery later said. "I mean, it didn't seem logical that this would happen. But we didn't know for sure." Physician Mike Kiernan gave a similar account. "I was really scared, although I couldn't show it at the time," he said. "For all we knew, all of Lake Pontchartrain was going to pour into the city and the water was going to rise so high that we couldn't even get from the hospital to our parking garage. [The walkway connecting the two was on the second floor.] Then we would have really been stuck."

In the middle of all this chaos and fear, the hospital staff got an unexpected and welcome addition. In one of the most remarkable stories that came out of the entire week, a pediatric critical care doctor named Leron Finger made his way back into downtown New Orleans and to Tulane Hospital, culminating a journey that had started that morning in Houston. Finger had left New Orleans for Texas Sunday morning with his wife, then stared at television reports of the hurricane all Sunday night and early Monday morning. After the storm passed, he began worrying about his patients back in New Orleans. "I made some calls and was able to get through to a FEMA [Federal Emergency Management Agency] representative in Baton Rouge," said Finger. "That man said that they were going to send a convoy of buses and police vehicles into New Orleans in a few hours, and if I could get there they'd take me along. So I went to Wal-Mart, bought a flashlight, a plastic rain jacket, some power bars, and some bottled water, and I set off for Baton Rouge."

When he got to Baton Rouge, Finger found the convoy and made friends with a Louisiana state trooper named Ritchie Stanley. And, as it turns out, Stanley's younger sister had been treated for cystic fibrosis nearly twenty years earlier by Dr. Robert Beckerman, Tulane's chief of pediatric pulmonology. "[Beckerman] is a very close friend of ours, and he helped train Dr. Finger, and so we got to talking," Stanley said months later. "I told him to ride down in my car."

Stanley drove Finger into New Orleans, passing roadblocks that were halting civilians trying to make their way back into the city. "We saw tons of debris and devastation along the way, and of course when we got to New Orleans many of the routes were closed because of the hurricane and because the water was rising," Finger said. Officer Stanley, obviously an expert on back roads and on New Orleans' topography, found his way to Tulane Hospital, at one point walking out of the car to make sure the water wasn't too deep for his vehicle to pass through. As he later explained: "There was no radio communication to speak of by this time, and it was very dark, and we pretty much had to make our own way into the city. We just had to find the highest ways to get through."

At around one a.m., Stanley's patrol car dropped off Dr. Finger within walking distance of Tulane Hospital. With water up to his knees, he made his way to the hospital building, explained who he was to security, and entered the building. "I said hi to everyone, and they were all very shocked because I was the first person they had seen from the outside world."

By this time water had risen to such levels that Stanley nearly didn't make it to the Superdome. "I had a chain saw in my trunk and had to fire it up to move some trees so I could get where I was going," he said. For the next twenty-two hours he drove back and forth from Baton Rouge to New Orleans, ferrying supplies and people into the flooded city. "I must admit that later on, when I realized just how flooded the city was, I wondered whether Dr. Finger would hate me for life for taking him back into the city that night," Stanley said.

On the contrary. "Officer Stanley was my guardian angel," Finger said.

Many HCA hospitals have helipads, but Tulane wasn't one of them. Installing one had been discussed many times. But, like every other hospital in downtown New Orleans, Tulane used the helipads at the Louisiana Superdome when helicopter travel was necessary. This, of course, was not an option after the Katrina flood.

Discussions about a helipad had centered on one of Tulane's two parking garages, called the Saratoga Street Parking Garage. It seemed large enough for a helicopter, and a structural engineer had once declared it strong enough to hold a helicopter. But the various steps to turn the top floor of the garage into an operating and Federal Aviation Administration-approved helicopter landing pad had never been taken.

On Monday afternoon, when many of Tulane's staffers were venturing outside to take a glimpse at the post-Katrina damage, hospital CEO Jim Montgomery began to contemplate the need for an air evacuation. "I went up to the roof of the garage when the wind was still blowing just to look it over," Montgomery said. "I'm not sure why I did this, to be honest, because at the time it didn't look like we needed to evacuate, and certainly not by air. But I wanted to take a mental picture of what the place looked like. And I went up there and noticed there were four light poles that would have to come down if we were ever going to land an aircraft up there."

In one of those weird coincidences, Montgomery had played golf only a few days earlier with a representative of Acadian Ambulance Service Inc., a Lafayette, Louisiana-based firm that owned seven helicopters. "I used to be head of another hospital that once sold its ambulance service to Acadian, so I had known them for years," Montgomery said. At about four or five in the morning of Tuesday, August 30, with water rising all over the city of New Orleans, Montgomery and Lagarde decided it was time to start evacuating patients. "We called Acadian and asked them to get there as soon as they could," Montgomery said.

Montgomery later reflected on the ironic timing of this decision. "Almost exactly thirty years earlier – in August 1975 – I had started my residency at Tulane Medical School. And here I was on that same day making the decision to start evacuating patients."

Mike Sonnier, air services coordinator for Acadian, fielded the call and reacted quickly. "I already had helicopters on the way to New Orleans, and I diverted a couple of them over to the hospital," he said.

"We didn't have much time to think about this, so we just did it. The next thing I knew they were calling me from the deck of the parking garage."

Acadian eventually devoted all of its helicopters to the evacuation (although on that first day they were only able to send three). In aircraft nomenclature, they were BO-105s, which are configured for advanced life support and can haul two patients in addition to the pilot and medic.

About the same time Montgomery called Acadian, his colleagues began alerting other HCA hospitals that they would soon be getting Tulane patients by airlift. Among the people awakened by Kim Ryan between three and five a.m. that day were Deborah Spell, chief nursing officer at Southwest Medical Center, and Leona Boullion, chief nursing officer at Women's and Children's Hospital. (Both facilities were located in Lafayette, Louisiana, about a two-hour drive under normal conditions.) "She told me New Orleans was flooding, they would lose power in only a few hours, and they would be evacuating their patients out of there," Boullion recalled. "I told her immediately that we could at least take all their babies and their kids. And she told me she'd call me back. So I woke up and got to work."

At this point – in the stressful early hours of Tuesday morning – evacuation was only assumed necessary for Tulane's most critical patients. Since there was no sign of the flood waters subsiding, the idea that a lot of people might have to evacuate by air was already being discussed. But at the time it still seemed more likely that a mass evacuation of staff and family members would be carried out by bus. "We saw the huge National Guard trucks, and so we figured there must be a way in and out of the city," said physician Mike Kiernan. "We also knew there was dry land five or six blocks away."

Tulane's maintenance staff took down the four light poles, using a pickup truck and a strong chain. Then, within the command center, it was decided that Sharif Omar, the hospital's associate vice-president for operations, would be on the parking garage's top floor when the first helicopter came in. "I really didn't know anything about helicopters, but no one else knew anything about helicopters either," he said. "But part of my job is transporting patients, so I guess it seemed like a fit."

Meanwhile Acadian had said they were on their way, but there was one small detail they needed to know: the latitude and longitude of the destination. Naturally, this was a question to which no one knew the answer. "As it turns out, I had mapping software on my laptop because I am a Boy Scout leader," Kiernan said. "I turned it on, zoomed in on the corner of Tulane Avenue and LaSalle Street, and there it was." Figuring that some of the pilots might appreciate a "map" of the garage area, Kiernan went to the top floor after sunup and sketched the "helicopter pad," noting the direction of magnetic north and the location and relative height of nearby buildings. "We didn't have an operating fax machine, but I gave it to the first pilot who left and asked him to find a way to have copies faxed to any other pilots coming in," Kiernan said. As unscientific as the map was, some pilots would use it in the next few hours the first time they approached Tulane. "So that's where that sketch came from!" pilot John Holland said a few weeks later.

The appearance of New Orleans shocked everyone when the sun came up on Tuesday. By this time the water had reached a height of between two and four feet outside the hospital, depending on which direction you looked. Tulane was an island and would remain so for the next few weeks. Downtown's streets had vanished, and people were already beginning to wade past the hospital in the direction of the Superdome. "Normally in a city all the noise is coming from the streets," one person in the hospital said. "After the flood none of it came from the streets. It all came from helicopters in the air, and then the occasional gunshot from God knows where. It was a different place."

At about five a.m., water reached the height where Tulane's plant operations staff shut down the emergency backup generators fixed to the building. "We waited until right before water got to a level where it was going to get past the electrical switches that would have shut it down anyway," said plant operations director George Jamison. The tractor-trailer generator perched outside, which was originally intended to be a supplement to the fixed backup generators inside the building, was now the only source of power to the Tulane Hospital system, providing AC power to the red power switches and limited air conditioning on that first full day after the flood. Elevators also continued to operate, although the decision was made on Tuesday afternoon to stop using them because of a fear that flooding had rendered them unsafe.

Lagarde called the top officials at HCA at about six Tuesday morning. He made it clear to his boss (Sam Hazen, president of HCA's western group of hospitals) that the entire city of New Orleans was flooded and the facility needed more helicopters than he would be able to procure. The corporate office got to work helping Tulane with its evacuation.

Shortly after this hospital officials called a meeting of all physicians. In spite of attempts to instill confidence, the meeting conveyed an alarming tone. "I looked around the room and noticed everyone had a look of fear," wrote Steven Davidoff. "We were finally told that a levee had broken and that water had been rising since early that night (confirming what I knew). Next, we were told an evacuation was being planned. I wondered how you could ever plan to evacuate an entire hospital when you were crippled with fear, rising water, and soon-to-be-no electricity. I feared that without electricity our hospital would be crippled. After all, we depended on electricity to power all IVs, to run labs, and to ventilate patients."

Acadian Ambulance was on its way, but there was no way of knowing exactly when they would arrive. As soon as daylight broke, Sharif Omar climbed onto the roof of the garage and waited. There were other helicopters flying over New Orleans already, and Omar had no idea which one was coming to Tulane. "You'd see a helicopter coming, and the only way you knew that it was one of ours is that they'd hover over us for a second, then fly around to survey the area, and then come back again," he later said.

Despite not being the first company called, the first aircraft that arrived that day was from Airheart, the helicopter service owned by Sacred Heart Health System in Pensacola, Florida. It arrived at about eight a.m., at a time when Omar was the only person standing on the roof of the garage. "We weren't a hundred percent sure the garage could hold a helicopter, so we cleared the building except for me," he said. "I guess I was expendable." The aircraft landed, and the pilot explained that it had a nurse on board and it was configured for a neonatal patient. Tulane staffers carefully wheeled an incubator carrying a small baby out of her room on the fourth floor, down the hall, onto an elevator, then out onto the second floor, across the walkway, into the parking garage, then up the series of ramps to the top floor. (It would be several trips before the idea of using pickup trucks to ferry patients dawned on anyone.) The process took nearly an hour, when the helicopter finally lifted off on its way to the HCA-owned Women's and Children's Hospital of Lafayette. Thus, the first person was evacuated. "To me that was one of the best moments," Kiernan said. "When that first patient left, I thought, 'hey, we are going to do this!'"

Chapter Four
Babies and Kids

R elief or not, the lengthy evacuation of the first infant made clear how long the process would take. Throughout Saturday, Sunday, and Monday, Tulane's administrators were getting constant updates on patient counts and conditions. On Monday night, when water began to rise in the streets of New Orleans, the hospital had 120 patients (plus the fifty-eight patients from the Superdome). Only about half of the Tulane patients could walk or sit upright. Twenty-one patients were in critical condition.

There were twenty-eight infants or children among the patients. And although there were exceptions to the rule, infants and children were evacuated before the adults.

Many of the small children had at least one parent present at Tulane Hospital during Katrina. "My two-week-old daughter, who was on a ventilator, was one of the first babies taken out," said Steve Schaaf, who later caught a helicopter out from the Tulane garage. But there were exceptions. Heather Fallon had a four-month-old son at Tulane's neonatal intensive care unit who had just undergone heart surgery. With the hurricane bearing down on the Gulf Coast, she drove to Lucevale, Mississippi, to prepare her home for the storm. Fallon had a phone conversation with a nurse at Tulane at about three a.m. on Monday. From that point on, she couldn't get through by telephone. The next thing she heard, on Tuesday afternoon, her son had been airlifted to Women's and Children's Hospital in Lafayette. "We couldn't have asked for a better hospital," Fallon said months later.

Jill Williams, whose month-old daughter was also at Tulane's neonatal intensive care unit, was in a similar situation. When the hurricane bore down on New Orleans, she headed north to her parents' house in Amite, Louisiana. "I figured as soon as the hurricane came through I'd come back to New Orleans," she later said. After the storm came through, she too found it impossible to get a phone call through to Tulane. On Tuesday she learned that her daughter had been transferred to Women's and Children's Hospital. "Now that I look back on it, I realize how lucky I was," said Williams, whose home in the New Orleans suburb of Metairie was relatively undamaged.

Most of the helicopters transporting infants out on Tuesday had medical personnel on board, but some did not – necessitating that a doctor or nurse go with the baby. On Tuesday afternoon two Tulane nurses left in the company of two infant patients. The helicopter landed in Baton Rouge to refuel, then continued on to Rapides Regional Medical Center in Alexandria, Louisiana. As one of the nurses, Christina Riviere, disembarked from the helicopter, the baby clinging to her, an Associated Press photographer took a photograph of her (the cover shot of this book). "I was exhausted at the time, but I had no idea then how long it would be before my colleagues at Tulane made it out like I did," Riviere said months later.

The neonatal patients had all been evacuated by about three o'clock that day. Focus then shifted to pediatric patients and adult patients in critical condition.

Of course, getting patients away from Tulane Hospital and flooded New Orleans was only half the problem. Federal law maintained that a hospital couldn't legally discharge a patient who still needed medical treatment until they had first found a receiving hospital for that patient. Tulane may have been the only New Orleans-area hospital that managed to comply with this law during the week following Hurricane Katrina.

The hospital was largely able to do so by transferring its patients to HCA's other hospitals in the region. Among the HCA hospitals that admitted Tulane patients during the week were Lakeview Regional Medical Center in Covington; Women's and Children's Hospital in Lafayette; Rapides Regional Medical Center in Alexandria; Medical City Hospital in Dallas; and HCA Methodist in San Antonio. And, in the chaos of the week, there were Tulane patients who ended up at other medical institutions. One patient, for instance, ended up at Our Lady of the Lake Regional Medical Center in Baton Rouge.

Finding hospitals to transfer patients to could be difficult. On Tuesday morning, Dr. Leron Finger – the physician who had made his way back into New Orleans after the hurricane – began arranging the evacuation of a teenage boy with a traumatic leg injury. Knowing the boy could only be treated at certain facilities, he called an official with Texas Children's Hospital and woke him up at about 4 a.m. "I don't think he realized the magnitude of the situation because I'm pretty sure he hadn't heard yet about the flooding," Finger said. "But nevertheless when I explained the situation to him, and told him I had six kids in intensive care and 15 others who weren't, he said he could definitely take the boy with the leg injury, and that I would need to call back on the other kids." Eventually, all of Tulane's pediatric patients (other than those in the neonatal intensive care unit) would be transferred to Texas Children's.

This process was made far more complicated by the fact that all of these hospitals were being inundated with patients who originated with every other hospital in the New Orleans area. "We probably had thirty or forty different helicopters carrying patients land here that week, and most of the time they weren't carrying a patient from Tulane," said Max Lauderdale, CEO of Lakeview. "We got patients from Methodist and Chalmette and all sorts of places. Sometimes the patients wouldn't have a medical record or anything, and we'd take them into the hospital and triage them and treat them if we needed to, or send them to another hospital in Baton Rouge or somewhere." Leona Boullion, the chief nursing officer at Women's and Children's Hospital in Lafayette, said her hospital either admitted or assisted in the evacuation of fifty-two children that week. "Before then if you had told me we were going to do that, I probably would have fainted," she said.

Some Tulane patients posed unusual logistical challenges. Two of them were so obese that moving them from the hospital to the helicopter, and moving them on the helicopter itself, would be a challenge. There were two patients awaiting heart transplants, both of them completely dependent on electrically-powered, four-hundred-pound machines that pumped their hearts. One of the patients was fifteen years old, the other thirty.

The task of telling individual patients about the evacuation was left to doctors and nurses. Considering the situation, this process went smoothly. The courage shown by pediatric patients was especially noteworthy. "The kids were sort of interesting," Marta Rozans said. "They sort of recognized that the situation was bad, and their moms were a bit scared, and somehow many of them knew if they got scared, mom was going to get even more scared. So a lot of them were stoic to protect their parents."

The more difficult part, Rozans said, was explaining to the parents that all patients were going to be evacuated before any parents were. "That was, for me, one of my scariest moments – telling the parents they couldn't go with their children on the helicopters," she said. This process was made all the more traumatic by the fact that, for many parents, it happened very quickly. "I'll never forget it," said Robin Norwood, whose three-year-old son had cancer and was at the hospital awaiting a bone marrow transplant. "About 5:30 or 6 in the morning they came running up the stairs telling us to bring the kids now. So we all ran down to the parking garage, and I'm carrying my son. Somewhere along the way they told me that my child was going but I wasn't."

With the parents temporarily saying goodbye to their children, there was an understandable concern that they might lose track of their kids, or that their kids might end up at a different hospital than intended. Rozans said they came up with an innovative and low-tech way to address that concern. "We got out pens and wrote all over these kids," she said. "We wrote on their backs, across their faces, on their arms, whatever. We wrote, 'I belong at Texas Children's Hospital.' And then we also had them write phone numbers on the children's bodies – not the parents' number, because they were with us, but the number of a good family friend in another part of the country who knew what was going on."

People react differently in crisis situations. Although the vast majority of patients, staff, and family members reacted calmly and positively to what they were asked to do during the days after the flood, there were ugly scenes. On at least one occasion, goes one story, a man was so reluctant to let his wife go on a helicopter without him that he only agreed to do so after being threatened. There were also a small number of Tulane employees who decided to leave the hospital on foot. "I know some people put their stuff on their heads and waded out into the water," plant operations manager George Jamison said. Interviewed about two months after the flood, Jamison said, "I have no idea what became of them."

Those who experienced the ordeal later pointed to several things that kept their morale high. One way was to drink plenty of fluids. The hospital had several days' supply of water already, and helicopters frequently brought water with them when they landed to get patients. In fact, at no time did anyone at Tulane apparently feel the need to hoard water. "I for one wasn't too crazy about the idea of using kitty litter and red plastic bags," chief nursing officer Danita Sullivan said. "So I just drank enough water to keep going, and no more." Fourteen-year-old Sam Rozans had a similar idea. "I was very careful not to eat or drink anything that contained fiber," he later said. "So I didn't eat granola bars. I knew what fiber would make me do."

Another morale booster was the ability to keep in touch with loved ones elsewhere – which was easier for some people than it was others. Carla Staxrud was an emergency medical technician with Guardian Emergency Medical Services who found herself stranded at Tulane Hospital after the flood. Before the hurricane she sent her seven-year-old son out of New Orleans with his father. But through Monday, Tuesday, and most of Wednesday, she was unable to get in touch with them or find out where they went. Finally, on Wednesday, she got the message (from her parents in California) that her son was safe. "I was in tears I was so happy," she later said. "And I'll never forget it, because at that exact moment one of my fellow EMTs broke down and started crying in a panic because she had just learned that she was going to fly out on a helicopter, and she was afraid of flying.

"Fortunately there were a lot of doctors around and there was a pharmacy, so they took care of her. But for those few moments we must have looked like quite a pair, both crying."

Staxrud said the main way to keep from getting down was to stay busy. "I was very happy to have work to do," she said. "We carried a lot of babies down several flights of stairs and then over to the parking garage and then up all the ramps to waiting helicopters," she said. "I remember at one point that my partner Thomas was carrying two babies from the NICU, one in each arm. I was carrying their IVs, and two nurses were carrying their charts."

Another person who stayed busy was fourteen-year-old Sam
Rozans, the son of Dr. Marta Rozans. "He didn't want to just twiddle his
thumbs, so he worked non-stop around the clock," his mother proudly
said a few weeks later. "He helped move mattresses, and he ran laboratory specimens and results up and down the stairs because the elevators
weren't working. And when the helicopters started coming and bringing
supplies he carried those as well, things like cartons of water. He was constantly moving."

Of course, staying busy is an easy remedy for a staff member, or a
family member of a staff member. But most of the patients and their family members couldn't stay busy. And, for the most part, they didn't panic
either. "I think the main thing that helped was that we talked to them,"
Kim Ryan said. "The only time there was some bedlam, as I remember
it, was when the lights went out on Tuesday night. But we had flashlights
ready to go, and we just calmly told everyone what was happening.

"As long as they knew we had a plan, and as long as they could see
that the staff wasn't panicking, they were OK."

People were also kept busy by taking part in one of the many dramatic subplots taking place within the hospital. None was as exciting as
the evacuation of the fifteen-year-old boy who needed a new heart.
After many phone calls, Dr. Leron Finger arranged for him to be flown by
helicopter to Lafayette, Louisiana, and then by fixed-wing aircraft to Texas
Children's Hospital in Houston, Texas. Since the young man had to be
transported along with a large cardiac-assist machine, getting the right helicopter was part of the logistical challenge – but not the hardest part. The
patient's room was on the fourth floor of the hospital. Somehow, boy and
machine had to be carried down two flights of stairs, then moved across the
walkway to the parking garage, then up the series of ramps in the parking

garage to the top floor, and then loaded into the helicopter.

This required a lot of forethought. Under normal conditions, the idea of disconnecting a patient from the machine keeping him alive – even for a few minutes – would be unthinkable. But there was no way to pull off this logistical move without doing just that, which meant that the big machine would go down on one trip and the boy would be carried down on another, escorted by the nurse operating the hand-pump mechanism.

Executing the evacuation was made all the more difficult by the fact that it was dark – pitch dark – both inside and outside the facility. It took until around eleven p.m. on Tuesday night for the special helicopter to arrive to take the boy away. About three hours earlier, the tractor-trailer generator that had been providing limited electrical power to the hospital ran out of diesel fuel, and the hospital was thrown into complete darkness. From then on, other than battery-operated devices, the only things operating on power at the hospital were charged by portable generators. In addition to everything else, this created a security problem, since many of the interior and exterior locks at Tulane Hospital were electrically powered and could not lock when the power went out.

From the roof of the parking garage it was possible to hear occasional gunfire, although no one could know – or would ever know – who was shooting and at what they were shooting. "All the other flights had been called off, but that kid was a special run and we couldn't call that off," said Omar. "So that night, we drove four cars from elsewhere in the parking garage to the roof, knowing that when we heard the helicopter, we could light up the top of the garage with headlights. Then we sat there on the roof in the darkness and waited.

"I must tell you we were a bit nervous at this point. Keep in mind that there are hotels all around us, and for all we know some of the gunfire is coming from a room in one of those hotels. We must have sat up there for an hour and a half in the pitch dark. Finally we heard a helicopter coming and we turned the headlights and our flashlights on, and then it must have done eight pass-overs."

Once the aircraft landed, the process of moving patient and machine began. Moving the boy and pumping the hand-mechanism weren't huge problems, since the teenager being moved was showing a tremendous amount of courage. But it took many strong men to move the machine down the dark stairs. In a process largely directed by EMTs, ropes were tied around the machine, and the machine gently lowered one step at a time. "I think there were eleven of us who actually did it," said Byron Brimmer, a respiratory therapist. "I can only say that the thing weighed a ton." Finger, who had helped make arrangements for the boy to be evacuated, watched nervously. "I weigh about 145 pounds, and so I'm not one of the really strong guys," he later said. "So I held a flash-light."

Somehow they were able to get the machine down the stairs, across the second floor bridge to the parking garage, and onto a pickup truck. A group of people held the boy's wheelchair in place on the drive up the ramp. "He was wide awake, and I remember how big his eyes were," said Carla Staxrud, an EMT who rode in the back of the truck. "One of the guys on my crew was trying to keep him calm by distracting him and ask-ing him questions. I remember him saying, 'So, you got a girlfriend?' But I am sure the sight of all of us helping to get him up there all tense and everything didn't help any."

When everyone reached the helicopter, another obstacle had to be overcome: the machine was slightly too large to fit in the helicopter door. Fortunately someone had a screwdriver handy. They removed its wheels, and the machine slid in.

Many cheered when the helicopter carrying the fifteen-year-old heart patient departed. "Everyone was crying and hugging each other," said Staxrud. When Dr. Finger got back to the hospital, he saw the other patient awaiting a new heart (who was thirty years old). "He shook my hand and said, 'Doc, thanks for getting him out,'" Finger said later. "I was kind of overwhelmed. I mean, here is this guy who has no idea if he is going to survive, and he was thanking us for getting the other guy out first. That truly was one of the most remarkable moments for me of the whole week."

By this time it was around midnight. There would be no more flights until the sun came up Wednesday.

Viewed one way, things seemed dreadful at Tulane Hospital. A few hours earlier, as the flood waters rose, no one could give an accurate and certain explanation of what was causing it or when the water would subside. There was always the possibility that the flood waters would subside within a day or so. But as Tuesday passed, it became clear that the flooding was caused by broken levees, and that water would be around for a while. "When the first helicopter came in, the pilot told us there was water everywhere and it looked like it was coming in from a levee break," Lagarde said. "At that point people began waking up and using their cell phones to call people who were watching the news. They were able to tell us what was going on."

Since there was no running water, and since there was no way to control and regulate where every person was using the bathroom, parts of the building were beginning to reek. "The city sewer system was obviously backing up and spilling out and creating an acrid smell that over the next few days made it almost impossible to breathe," Jim Montgomery later wrote. "And, of course, with no water pressure you can't bathe.

"But here's a general observation: if everyone smells the same you really don't notice it. You just feel unclean."

The building was dark, except where people had flashlights. The heat was awful. "I was sweating from head to toe the entire time I was there," said Cheryl Turano. "We cut off our jeans to stay cooler."

Occasional gunfire could be heard in the distance, reminding the hospital's small security staff – many of whom got little sleep that week – of just how important their job was. "We were always kind of worried that someone might sneak onto a stairwell and make their way into the hospital looking for drugs, or that someone in a building near us might shoot at us for whatever reason," said Warren Breaux, Tulane's deputy chief of police. "Now, that may sound far-fetched, but there are a lot of people who feel like they need drugs. And keep in mind that we could see people walking around in buildings adjacent to us with flashlights. Not a good sign."

No one was comfortable. "I remember that after a while everyone started walking funny because they were chafed in the same spot," said Carla Staxrud. "It was hot and muggy, and you were wearing the same underwear you had been in for days, and it kept rubbing in the same places. Meanwhile a lot of people were getting blisters because their feet were wet and they had been walking around all day."

Perhaps most dreadful of all, just about everyone at Tulane Hospital had someone else to worry about. Some people hadn't heard from family members since the hurricane hit. Some had relatives staying at the Park Plaza Hotel two blocks away. And, of course, the general situation in the city of New Orleans was depressing, especially to people who call the city home. There is nothing that compares to the despair of seeing your home city destroyed.

However, on the bright side, an estimated sixty-three patients had been evacuated that day – half of them in critical condition. Everyone in the hospital was safe. There was plenty of water and plenty of food. In spite of the large number of people in the hospital, it was still possible to find an empty corner of the building where you could lie down, curl up, and sleep for an hour or two.

Perhaps there was no better sign of the human spirit, influenced by the culture of New Orleans, than the following anecdote: On Tuesday night, after the fifteen-year-old heart patient had safely been evacuated, a group of Tulane's surgeons held a small toga party in the pre-op area. Months later, none of the doctors and nurses who attended the event would comment on where the alcohol came from. "Some things that happen in New Orleans need to stay in New Orleans," one physician said.

Chapter Five
Helicopters and Roadblocks

W hen Mel Lagarde called his boss in Nashville and explained the situation at Tulane Hospital, it set into motion a series of events within HCA. As staff at the corporate headquarters heard about Tulane's plight, they reacted swiftly. The first priority was to get everyone out. To achieve this, there were dozens of immediate problems to be tackled at once: get as many helicopters as possible to participate in the evacuation; get water, food, equipment, and additional fuel to Tulane; find hospital beds for the patients being evacuated and help coordinate the evacuations where needed; get twelve-hundred staff members, staff members' families, and patients' families away from the hospital to a place where they would be safe, and a place where they could be cared for if they, too, needed medical attention; find accommodations for all these people; help people at Tulane communicate with their loved ones; and coordinate all these efforts. There was also the need to comply with federal regulations, such as the one requiring patient information be kept private in the midst of the crisis.

Response from corporate headquarters went all the way to the top of the company. "By the time I got to work Tuesday morning, Sam [Hazen] was already in the board room with everyone else, and as soon as I got there they made the situation apparent to me," said Jack Bovender, CEO of HCA. "I think Mel was actually on speakerphone at that exact moment. He was telling us where the flood waters were and how long they thought it would be until they lost the generators. Our main focus immediately became how to get those patients out."

Tulane was HCA's most formidable problem, but it wasn't the company's only concern. The nation's largest hospital company had several hospitals hit by Hurricane Katrina, including Garden Park Medical Center in Gulfport, Mississippi; Lakeview Regional Medical Center in Covington, Louisiana; Lakeside Hospital in Metairie, Louisiana; and DePaul-Tulane Behavioral Heath Center in New Orleans.

In fact, in the immediate wake of Katrina, the most damage by far appeared to be at Garden Park, a 136-bed facility. "Garden Park had been really smacked by the eye of the storm," Sam Hazen said. "There was much more damage to Garden Park's structure and the community around it from the hurricane than to Tulane and New Orleans, or so we thought. On Monday Garden Park badly needed us to send them water and fuel and supplies and security, and it wasn't easy to get things in because the area was so devastated."

When the Tulane crisis occurred, the task of finding helicopters fell to Ed Jones, head of supply for HCA's Eastern Group of hospitals, and to Chuck Hall, head of HCA's North Florida division. Much of it was then delegated to David Smith, director of contracting for the north Florida division. "Chuck Hall called me into the conference center and told me we needed helicopters to evacuate Tulane," Smith said. "'How many?' I asked him. 'I don't know,' he said. 'Where will they be taking all these patients?' I asked. 'I don't know,' he said. And that was when it all started for me.

"Fortunately I had a file of some of these companies. I just opened it up and went to the Internet and started going from one company to another."

Among the firms Smith was able to hire within a few hours were Airheart of Pensacola; Baptist Hospital of Pensacola; LifeNet (a division of Colorado-based Air Methods Corp.); Missouri-based Air Evac Lifeteam Inc.; St. Louis Helicopter LLC; and Houston Helicopters Inc.

Sometimes the connections were complicated. For example, Ed Jones called some of HCA's major suppliers and asked them for help. One of those suppliers, Chicago-based equipment distributor Medline, had an executive named Bill Abington. Abington had met someone who owned a helicopter used in a law enforcement capacity by the Winthrop Harbor (Illinois) police department. Abington called Dan Bitton, a Vietnam veteran and the police department's head pilot, and as soon as possible the twin-engine EC-135 was headed south. "It took us five hours and thirty-six minutes to fly down," Bitton later said. "We landed at Acadian's facility in Lafayette and unloaded a lot of the gear we had in the back. We also took three seats out, which left two back there. They loaded me up with bottled water and medical supplies. And we headed into the darkness to find Tulane."

As HCA's corporate executives began signing up ambulance companies, fear that they would lose the assets they were hiring was always in the back of their minds. "We could see this national disaster developing on television, and we were always afraid companies like Acadian were going to get commandeered by the federal government," said Hazen. "We were always afraid our efforts would be shut off."

When the Tulane airlift was completed, HCA and its many hospitals would document lessons learned from the saga. One of the first was the need to carefully record official communications from the Tulane command center. "We had a million people calling in and a million things going on," said Richard Bracken, HCA's chief operating officer, who was in the corporate command center that entire week. "With all of this taking place, one of the first things that we realized was that we needed a spokesman when it came to talking to Tulane, and Sam [Hazen] became that person."

With phone coverage spotty at times, Bracken said it made sense to have regularly scheduled updates. "We made it a rule of thumb to have a phone conversation on the hour and every half hour, even if we weren't sure if there was something new to say. This ended up being hugely important."

One thing that became obvious as companies signed on to take part in the evacuation was that someone with helicopter expertise needed to take charge of the operation. John Holland, an experienced pilot with LifeNet, volunteered to do this, although at the time neither he nor anyone else knew exactly what this would entail. Early Wednesday morning he flew into New Orleans as a crew member on one of his company's aircraft. His first order of business was to secure fuel, and toward this effort he went straight to Louis Armstrong International Airport, just west of New Orleans. "I found a young man refueling, and he had half a tank of gas there and an entire five thousand gallon tank elsewhere at the airport. I told him to go ahead and hold some of it and that I would pay for it."

At that time, Holland assumed he would be piloting missions in and out of downtown New Orleans on a rotating twelve-hour shift with one of his peers. But he changed his mind, he said, when he and some of his colleagues arrived at Tulane later that morning.

> When we landed, we shut down our two machines and [director of pediatric services] Kim Graham [who had begun working on the parking garage with Sharif Omar] took us downstairs. When we got down to the second deck of the parking garage, there were tons of patients and people; they had gotten

them out of the hospital because of the heat. There were maybe thirty to fifty people lying on the concrete and on chairs, and you could just see the look of desperation in everyone's eyes. I'm thinking to myself, 'This is really, really bad.'

So we go into the building. It was really dark, even in the daytime, because there were no lights. And we go down to the command post or whatever they were calling it. They had one little battery-operated lamp lighting up the room with people standing around it, so you had this glow in the middle. I introduce myself and the first thing I ask them is whether they had any communications. And they told me the phones had just started working again, which obviously struck me as strange. So I called Dave Smith from there. And I remember that when I was on the phone with Dave, they relayed that they needed lots of D batteries, because all they had left was flashlight power.

Tulane officials asked Holland to stay with them to help coordinate the airlift. He did as they asked, and LifeNet medical director Stiles Clarke, who had flown in on the same helicopter with Holland, also agreed to stay. Within half an hour or so the two men were back on the roof of Tulane's parking garage, teaching Omar and Graham proper hand signals. "I gave them about a month's worth of training in a few minutes," Clarke said. "They learned fast."

I n an undertaking as large as the Tulane Hospital evacuation, it was inevitable that some things would go wrong. For one thing, there was HCA's attempt to get additional diesel fuel and gasoline to Tulane.

As mentioned earlier, HCA officials were aware that the emergency generators were fixed at a low elevation inside Tulane Hospital. Knowing this, the company had shipped a tractor-trailer-size generator to Tulane in advance of Hurricane Katrina. There was only enough diesel fuel on site to operate the generator for about fifteen hours. But HCA had staged a twenty-one-thousand-gallon diesel fuel tank at Lakeview Regional Hospital in Covington, with plans to shuttle tractor-trailers carrying fuel to facilities in need after the storm.

On Wednesday morning a tractor-trailer carrying three thousand gallons of diesel fuel left Lakeview Hospital en route to Tulane. With the Lake Pontchartrain Causeway shut down, driver Howard Myers headed west on Interstate 12, then south on I-55, then east on I-10. Since HCA knew roadblocks were set up along I-10, company government relations director David Critchlow had tried to make arrangements for a National Guard escort to meet Myers at one of the checkpoints and subsequently escort him to Tulane. But these weren't normal times. And it wasn't easy to figure out who to talk to in order to obtain a right of clearance for an eighteen-wheeler full of diesel fuel that day.

Once he got on I-10, Myers made it past the first few roadblocks. "At every checkpoint I'd tell them who I was and what I was doing, and I'd tell them that a Major So and So was supposed to be there to escort me into town," he said. "At every checkpoint they'd let me go on through because I was carrying fuel. And they'd tell me that maybe the major would be at the next checkpoint, but they said they knew nothing about it."

Myers made it all the way to the intersection of I-10 and the Lake Pontchartrain Causeway, where he saw a sea of evacuees waiting to get on buses to leave the city. "I think most of them were people who had been at the Superdome," he said. There, Myers was told he could not proceed any further without a National Guard escort. "They said they knew nothing about me or about a fuel truck trying to get to Tulane," he said. Myers pulled his rig to the side of the road and had a cellular phone conversation with Critchlow, who was working hard to get Myers cleared. Soon his vehicle was drawing attention from several evacuees, some of whom began climbing on his vehicle and asking for a ride. "Finally, this dude came up to the truck and asked me if I could get him out of there," Myers said. "Then he pulled out a gun and waved it at me, and I decided it was time to leave."

HCA's corporate office then began making intricate plans to fly the fuel to the hospital. "We were going to bring in two hundred gallons of fuel by helicopter and then have it poured into drums on the roof of the parking garage," said Ed Jones, who developed the nickname "Chopper Ed" within HCA circles as a result of that week. "We even found a company that could do it." The company was St. Louis Helicopters, which had three aircraft en route to New Orleans on Wednesday afternoon. Greg Miller, a pilot with St. Louis Helicopter, confirmed that his original mission was going to be delivering fuel. "But to be honest, we weren't sure how we were going to accomplish this," he later said. "Before we got down there the mission had been scrapped, and I started evacuating people instead." By this time HCA had decided it made more sense to focus all of its efforts on getting everyone out as soon as possible rather than to spend a day or more in a difficult attempt to send in more fuel.

Then there was the snafu related to one of the helicopters HCA hired, or, more accurately, tried to hire to assist in the evacuation. Through David Whalen, the CEO of an HCA hospital in Niceville, Florida, Smith learned about a privately owned Russian-built helicopter, owned by VSC, a firm based in Oregon. HCA asked VSC to join the airlift, and VSC agreed. But there was a problem: the Federal Aviation Administration, which had to clear all flights over New Orleans, would not authorize the MI-8 to fly over the city. "We tried and tried to get that thing cleared but we never pulled it off," said Smith. "We called that thing the 'Vladimir,' and that became our battle cry, kind of like, 'Will Vladimir fly today?'"

HCA never did get the straight story on why the FAA wouldn't let "Vladimir" fly. The most logical (and least cynical) explanation was that the aircraft was considered experimental in nature and had not passed the usual bureaucratic hurdles for clearance in such a situation. By the time the FAA approved the use of the MI-8, Tulane's evacuation was complete.

Chapter Six
Last Resort

Hundreds of Tulane's staff and family members of staff were at the Park Plaza Hotel in downtown New Orleans during Hurricane Katrina. There were also a few people associated with HCA's DePaul-Tulane Behavioral Health Center staying at the hotel. When the flood came, the Park Plaza became an island with no electricity, no running water, little communication with the outside world, and no sense of order.

Most of the Tulane-associated people staying at the hotel eventually made their way to the Saratoga garage, where they were airlifted out on Thursday and Friday. Some of the most traumatic first-person accounts of Hurricane Katrina came from these people.

When Katrina hit, Tulane physician Bob Ascuitto was working at Tulane Hospital. His wife, physician Nancy Ross-Ascuitto, was staying at the hotel with their fourteen-year-old son Michael and five-year-old daughter Susana. On Tuesday, Bob Ascuitto was heavily involved in helping his patients evacuate. He then waded into the flood water to fetch his family.

A few weeks after the ordeal, Bob and Nancy Ascuitto wrote accounts *of their experiences for the professional publication* Congenital Cardiology Today.

Here are excerpts:

FROM NANCY ROSS-ASCUITTO

The hotel was filled with people. In addition to 120 Tulane employees and their families, there were hundreds of New Orleanians, and many tourists seeking shelter from the storm. We had to step over people in the hallways and stairwells to move about.

It was obvious when the hurricane slammed into New Orleans. The city immediately darkened by loss of power. Hurricane winds reached deafening proportions. Windows rattled and some cracked; crashing sounds were heard outside the hotel. Finally, the sky lightened, although the sun hadn't quite risen. My first sight was of world famous Canal Street, widest street and the main thoroughfare for countless activities. It now resembled a white water river. Rapids and waves roared down the avenue, pushed along by unrelenting winds. Chunks of buildings and other debris rained on the streets. Cars were flipped over, and power lines draped the city like tinsel. As the sun rose, a moving object caught my eye. I focused on the rain and was startled to see a man crawling along trolley tracks toward the hotel. He grabbed onto a telephone pole to keep from blowing away. The land phones were dead, but my cell phone was still working. I dialed 911 but to no avail. When I again looked through the window, the man had disappeared.

The hotel was dark, packed with people and getting warmer by the minute. We waited in line in a stairwell for about two hours to get a sweet roll and half a glass of orange juice. It was here that we met some of our fellow refugees. Most of the guests were from poor families who had no way of fleeing the city when they were ordered to evacuate. There were also out-of-towners who had been stranded by the storm; a family from

Manhattan, whose son was visiting Tulane's undergraduate campus; a couple from Brooklyn celebrating their first wedding anniversary; and a group of men from England working as soccer coaches for the summer.

The first floor of the hotel was flooded [but not nearly to the degree that it would be the next day, after the levees broke]. Security personnel were telling us that we could leave the hotel and wade to the Superdome, where we would receive food and shelter. Guests that left, however, would not be allowed back in the hotel. I vividly recalled the deplorable conditions reported at the Superdome with the last hurricane. We stayed.

The next day was Tuesday. I knew the levees had broken; nothing else could have caused what we saw. Water had risen to the top of mailboxes. Many car roofs seen the day before were no longer visible. We went to the hotel roof to get a better view of the city. It was here that we saw the true devastation of the storm. Water covered the streets and the first floor of buildings in every direction. It is hard to imagine an entire city, a major city, submerged in water. Groups of people were huddled on the few parts of the interstate highway that were not under water. Even more shocking was the scene in the streets. Families were wading through chest-deep water, pushing their belongings on pieces of wood and plastic, makeshift rafts and an occasional small boat. Children were being floated down streets in boxes or containers. Some elderly were dragged through the water. These people were moving in the direction of the ill-fated Superdome. Some were yelling or gesturing to an occasional passing boat for help. The boats simply sped by them, leaving the people in their wake. On a raft, a man was towing a lifeless body. I told my children to look away.

The mood at the hotel was becoming increasingly tense. After another long wait in the now stifling stairwell, we were given one sandwich per person by hotel personnel. Guests started arguing with the staff for more food. People began shoving each other in the food line. I hurried the children back to our room. On our way back, a hotel official asked me if I were a physician (I was wearing surgical scrubs). She told me of a woman who desperately needed dialysis; perhaps I could help. Another woman, who was eight months pregnant, inquired if she could come to my room if she went into labor. Others asked me what diseases they could catch from being in the toxic water. I did the best I could, but what good is a physician without equipment, medicine, electricity or running water? For the remainder of the day, I and the children shared a can of soup, some peanut butter, and a small bottle of water.

The following day was Wednesday. We didn't dare leave our room, because there appeared to be complete chaos in the hallways. A security officer began directing people to leave the hotel. The officer told us that the room door locks were no longer working, and that water was continuing to rise in the hotel. The hotel was no longer able to provide food and was unable to protect us. She said that if we stayed in the hotel "we might die" and advised us to wade into the streets and flag down boats. Sure, I remembered the people in the water begging to be picked up by boats, but to no avail. We suddenly ran into the men [fellow guests] from England. They had waded through the chest-deep water four blocks to the Superdome only to be turned away. They did not look well.

This was the first time we felt our lives were truly in danger. We returned to the room and shared our last can of soup and bottle of water. My son said, "Mom, let's get out of here. I'll carry Suzy. We can make it." I marveled at his bravery.

Suddenly, [my husband] Bob's voice rang through the chaos. "Michael! Michael!" I couldn't believe it. How did he get here? I opened the door to see Bob in the hallway surrounded by hostile people. He confronted several of them, and they backed off.

FROM BOB ASCUITTO

I began receiving information that conditions at the hotel were rapidly deteriorating, with little food and water, no power, and people riot-ing. I decided to get my family out of that hell hole, ASAP. Hopefully I wasn't too late. As I raced to the water surrounding the hospital, I ran into one of our NICU nurses. She was trembling and very upset; her 80-year-old father with severe congestive heart failure and a recent stroke, elderly mother, and impaired daughter were staying at the hotel. She feared for their lives, and implored me to "please get them out." She insisted on coming with me, and frankly, I needed her to identify them. Somewhat reluctantly, I instructed her to take hold of my belt, as we slowly lowered ourselves into a chest-high soup of water, debris and fecal matter.

With each step I could feel the water clinging to my legs; it required an effort to simply move forward. To our left, draped over a twisted fence, was a downed power line. To our right a movement in the water sudden-ly caught my eye; it was a large black snake. I'm sure the snake was avoid-ing me as much as I was avoiding it. Thankfully the encounter proved uneventful. The unrelenting late-morning sun reflected off the water in front of us and made it appear bottomless. Nevertheless, we moved on and made it safely to the battered hotel.

We entered the hotel through a back door. The corridors were almost completely dark. Litter was everywhere. The lobby was under water. People, hardly discernable, were yelling and fighting, trying to get at remaining bits of food. Children were crying. Fortunately, during my youth, my brother and I learned much on the streets of northern New Jersey. I tensed my abdomen, clenched my fists, protected my head and fought my way up five flights of stairs. I emerged on the fifth floor with relatively minor injuries.

I started yelling, "Michael, Michael!" not knowing what room they were in, or whether they were in their room at all. "It's Dad, Michael!" Suddenly, at the end of the fifth floor hallway, the last door opened.

FROM NANCY ROSS-ASCUITTO

We moved out and started calling for other Tulane employees to follow. We found the daughter and elderly parents of our nurse. Another nurse and her family wanted to join us, but she couldn't find her mother. Bob told her to find as many people as she could and he would return for them.

We decided to go down a fire escape to avoid the fighting taking place in the stairwells. Bob led the way, carrying Suzy on his shoulders, and holding onto our nurse's daughter. Michael followed. The nurse helped her ailing father. I held onto the elderly woman, and led two other children down the fire escape. Other people began crying, but quickly followed.

The last half of the stairway disappeared into the putrid water. We hesitated at the water's edge, gathered our courage, and then plunged in. The water reached my chest, and the shoulders of the elderly woman. I could feel her hands shaking in mine. The water reeked of sewage and gasoline. We shuffled along taking tiny steps to avoid tripping. We heard gun shots behind us. We never looked back.

As we all followed Bob, my son said, "Mom, doesn't Dad look like Moses?" When we approached the hospital, shooting continued in the distance.

As we climbed out of the water, everyone breathed a sigh of relief. We had survived an unforgettable ordeal. Except for Suzy, we were soaking wet, and filthy. We left a trail of whatever debris we had picked up in the water. Michael, Suzy and I went to the medical school, where we cleaned ourselves with baby wipes soaked with disinfectant. Our clothes and shoes had to be thrown away. I tied rags to my feet to allow me to walk over broken glass we encountered. Bob returned to the hotel to lead another group of people back to the hospital. By noon our family was finally together.

Chapter Seven
Talking to Each Other

Hurricane Katrina took place in the era of the telephone, the cellular phone, the fax, Blackberry, Federal Express, and – of course – email. But the storm and the flood that followed it created a communication gap between the people in New Orleans and the rest of the country. It created a communication gap between the people in one part of New Orleans and the people in another. It even created a communication gap amongst the people in one part of Tulane Hospital and the people in another part of Tulane Hospital.

Since there was no time to plan this massive operation, and since the parking garage at Tulane Hospital had never served as a helicopter pad before, the order of the day was improvisation. It is easy to look back now and figure out how the operation could have gone more smoothly, and easy to come up with ways the company and the helicopters could have better talked to the people at Tulane. But these weren't normal times. And, looking back at the Tulane airlift, it is remarkable to note what worked, what didn't work, and what innovative solutions people devised.

Of about fifteen hundred people at Tulane Hospital when Hurricane Katrina hit, hundreds had cellular phones that were operable prior to the storm. However, the hurricane knocked out most cell phone coverage in the New Orleans area. For the rest of the week cell phones generally weren't very reliable. But some worked better than others. Many patients, staff, and family members spent the better part of that week checking and re-checking their cell phones in an attempt to get them to work. Sometimes, in the middle of the night, it might be possible to get a connection, even for a few minutes.

The existence of so many cell phones – unreliable as the service might have been – meant that there were erratic lines of communication between people in the hospital and points distant throughout the week. Some people were able to call their families to let them know how they were. In turn, many of them created phone or email chains to keep friends and family members of other people at Tulane informed of events there.

Cell phones also made it possible for people at Tulane to call the news media. On Wednesday doctors at Tulane Hospital helped notify Associated Press and CNN that Charity Hospital across the street had not been evacuated. That same day Tulane physician Jeff Myers spoke at length with National Public Radio, creating what ended up being the longest (and perhaps most accurate) national news story about events at the hospital. "I have been to third-world countries and I've been to Nicaragua and I've been to Africa, but I think the difference is the absolute fear here," Myers said on NPR. "People here haven't lived like this their whole lives. There is no adjustment to it.

"Every hour is going to continue to get worse. We hear gunfire, we hear everything. And one of our biggest fears is that every time the sun goes down things will get worse."

Meanwhile some of Tulane's land phone lines were surprisingly reliable. It may defy logic, but even after the city of New Orleans was flooded, land phone lines at Tulane Hospital were operative. On Tuesday night, when the tractor-trailer generator ran out of diesel fuel, the hospital's digital phone system (powered by electricity) went dead. But George Jamison, head of plant operations for Tulane, located two analog phone lines and receivers, giving the command center two working phones through most of Wednesday and Thursday. "I think George [Jamison] and the people who work for him deserve a lot of credit for this," said physician Mike Kiernan. "He was pulling miracles constantly.

"He was like Scotty [a character on *Star Trek*]. We'd have been in bad shape without the two phone lines that George kept running in and out of the command center. And I don't know how he did it. But the fact that we had those phone lines is one huge thing that distinguished us from Charity Hospital."

The analog phone lines didn't have a built-in long distance capability, creating a temporary quandary for Tulane officials. It was then that physician Bill Gill donated his AT&T calling card to the cause. "We couldn't make long distance calls, and for a while we weren't sure what we were going to do about it," Gill said. "I happened to have my AT&T calling card in my wallet, and I tried it and it worked. So I wrote the number down on two sheets of paper and put the number by the two phones.

"I haven't gotten my phone bill yet; I'm sure it'll be pretty high. But AT&T has told me they'll forgive the bill if I let them use that story."

There was another quirk about phone service in the flooded city. The infrastructure of New Orleans sustained such a blow from Katrina that it was practically impossible to make a local phone call. No one in the building was able to call Charity Hospital across the street, University Hospital across town, or the New Orleans police department. But people at Tulane were able to, with some reliability, call HCA's corporate headquarters, or a reporter, or a loved one.

Once the evacuation became inevitable, and helicopters began landing on Tulane's parking garage, the company needed a reliable communication system on the roof of the garage. In advance of such an emergency, HCA had stocked Tulane Hospital with satellite telephones that were supposed to provide such a function. But they didn't work as advertised. "We had trouble with those satellite phones the whole time," said Kiernan. "They don't seem to work in big cities surrounded by buildings, and this is one of the lessons that should come out of this. To get those things to work you had to get on the roof of the parking garage and hang off the edge of the building."

The company's solution to this problem was original. Richard Chase, maintenance director for HCA's Capital Regional Medical Center in Tallahassee, suggested the company contact Randy Pierce, emergency radio communications coordinator for the state of Florida. Pierce also happened to be a trustee for the Tallahassee Amateur Radio Society. And as it turns out, the Tallahassee Amateur Radio Society had a memorandum of understanding with Capital Regional under which HCA allowed the society to use its radio tower on the condition that the society help HCA in case of a communications emergency.

Before long, three members of the Tallahassee Amateur Radio Society (Theo Titus, Gene Floyd, and Bill Schmitt) were in Dave Smith's office at HCA in Tallahassee, all decked out in survivalist gear. "They were really into what they were doing," Smith later recalled. "They even introduced themselves to me by their call signs rather than their names." Pierce had equipped the operators with suitcase-size satellite radios, which he knew would work better than the satellite phones. After a bit of training, two of the three radio operators drove to Pensacola, where they took a helicopter to New Orleans (the third stayed in Tallahassee, where he would talk to the other two).

Like many of the people who contributed to the Tulane evacuation, these operators were volunteers. "They weren't paid, and they were told upfront that they weren't going to be paid," Pierce said. "This was all in the goodness of HAM radio and the goodness of the people of New Orleans. This is what we do. They volunteered to take a week out of work, go into harm's way, and work unbelievable hours in unbelievable conditions."

Titus, a sixty-four-year-old electrical engineer, got what he later described as a "crash course" in how to use the radios that Wednesday. "It's about twenty pounds or so, with a panel antenna at the top and the guts in the bottom," he later explained. "You tip the panel antenna up at a right angle and then you orient it towards the satellite, and the signal meter tells you whether you are locked in. Then you talk into it, and hopefully it works."

Titus and one of his colleagues then drove to Pensacola, where they boarded a helicopter that took them to Tulane. "We rode right down the Mississippi coast, a few hundred feet above the ground," he said. "The sight of it was heart-wrenching." Upon his arrival he got his radio to work, but he found he couldn't operate it on the top deck of the Saratoga garage. "The rotor blast was blowing my radio around," he said. "I ultimately ended up on Level Six of the garage, and they gave me a runner who stayed with me relaying messages back and forth for the next two days."

The second radio was stationed at Louis Armstrong Airport, where, by this time, HCA had decided to organize a staging area of sorts to coordinate the transfer of evacuees from helicopters to buses.

In the mass confusion of the airlift, there were differences of opinion as to whether the extra radio operators were effective. But according to HCA's office in Tallahassee, they were very beneficial. "I can assure you they were helpful," said David Smith. Starting Thursday, they were able to give HCA's Tallahassee office regular updates on the evacuation. Executives there took down every tidbit of information, and transformed a computer training classroom into something akin to a war room.

"There were five to seven of us basically living in that room for a week, with poster boards on the wall with phone numbers and contact names and satellite images and things like that," said Smith. "It was like a battle station. And there were pizza boxes lying around."

So thanks to cell phones, land phones, satellite radios, and volunteer HAM radio operators there was surprisingly good communication between HCA and Tulane Hospital. But this left another aspect of the communications world – the ability of Tulane to talk to the helicopters taking off and landing from its parking garage. In this regard, communication started badly and remained so the entire time. In fact, Tulane *never* had voice communication with the many helicopters involved in the airlift. "This is the thing about the helicopters that is important to understand," said Sharif Omar, who spent three days on the roof of the parking garage, communicating with the Tulane command center by walkie-talkie. "We might have known that a helo was on its way, but we didn't know if that meant it was two minutes away or forty-five minutes away. And often we didn't know that the helicopter flying overhead was going to land here. They would hover over us and do several passes and then we would know."

Had there been communication between people on the roof of the garage and the helicopters themselves, the process of loading and unloading would have gone faster. As it was, the staff at Tulane usually didn't know what a helicopter was capable of carrying until it landed. Some helicopters could carry several people, but all of them had to be sitting upright. Others were set up to carry critical patients, but usually a very small number at a time. "We did the best we could to send the critical patients first, in the order they should go, but what really drove triage was what kind of person the helicopter could take," said Kiernan. "And we didn't know what the helicopter could take until the pilot announced that he could only take a stretcher, or he could only take a baby, or he could only take people sitting upright, or whatever."

Once the aircraft were loaded, John Holland had a tried-and-true method of communicating where the helicopters needed to go. "I had a pad of paper and a pen and I would write down where they needed to take the patients," Holland said. "That seemed like the best thing, and it certainly made the most sense, because it was so loud up there you couldn't hear each other talk."

Although HCA officials didn't know it at the time, at least some of the helicopters were in communication with one another. On Wednesday, the Federal Aviation Administration asked Acadian Ambulance to assume control of the civilian medical evacuation of the New Orleans area, which meant pilots heading into New Orleans would check in with Acadian's air services coordinator Mike Sonnier. Sonnier put out the word that all helicopters flying in and out of Tulane should communicate with each other on VHF frequency 123.02. "Most everybody was monitoring that," said pilot Greg Miller. "But there wasn't a lot of chit-chat on there about how many patients you were carrying or where you were going or that sort of thing. It was just safety of flight stuff. If I saw someone circling to land, I might say their call sign and then, 'what are your intentions?' That sort of thing." Nevertheless, about half of the pilots interviewed for this book said they never knew there was an air-to-air frequency.

On Thursday Holland came up with a new plan. He began rounding up operable cellular phones from Tulane staffers and family members, asking everyone to put their name on the phone before they turned it in. Then he began giving three different cell phones (all of which were linked with a different cellular network) to each helicopter taking off from the garage that he knew would eventually be coming back. "I figured so long as we had cell phones on the roof of the garage, and cell phones in the air over New Orleans, this might help us a bit," Holland said.

Interviewed weeks later, Holland admitted he didn't know whether the cell phone to cell phone plan worked. "But I do at least think everyone got their phones back," he pointed out.

Chapter Eight
Chest-High

If there was a single image that dominated the coverage of Hurricane Katrina, it was the sight of New Orleanians carefully wading through the floodwater carrying what few possessions they could. People at Tulane Hospital and the Saratoga Street Parking Garage became familiar with this scene during the days after the Hurricane Katrina flood. Hundreds, maybe thousands, of strangers waded by Tulane Hospital. Some tried to make their way into the facility. With firmness, and a heavy heart, Tulane's security guards instructed them to keep moving. "We couldn't take everyone in – there was no way we could take everyone in," said CEO Jim Montgomery. "We told them to go to the Superdome. Everyone in the city knows where that is."

Most of the people at Tulane Hospital did not venture into the flood water. Those who did will never forget the experience.

Sonny Breaux, a supervisor for Tulane's maintenance department, was one of several Tulane staffers – like Dr. Bob Ascuitto – who had a room and a loved one at the Park Plaza Hotel. After the flood waters came, Breaux waded back and forth several times carrying food and water to his fiancée and some other family members of people he knew who were staying at the hotel. Breaux said the sanitary condition of the water was the least of his concerns. "You had to be careful not to step in a manhole or you would fall into it and die," he said. "You had to be careful not to step into fallen debris like telephone poles or trees or you could break your leg. And you had to be careful not to step onto fallen power lines because some of them were still hot and still moving."

Tyrone Augusta, director of facility services at DePaul-Tulane Behavioral Health Center, was one of three DePaul employees who had to rescue family members staying at the Park Plaza. On Tuesday evening, shortly before dark, they made several trips into and out of the hotel, where conditions were so bad, "I don't think I could even tell you about how bad they were," he later said. By the time he got to the hotel itself, he said, "the water was up to my neck." Once in the building, the first thing he noticed was that furniture was floating around the lobby. "There was a lot of looting going on, and I remember hearing it said that a thirteen-year-old girl had been raped," he recalled.

Some of the people Augusta and his colleagues rescued were calm; others were screaming and had to be carried outside, including an elderly woman. Once out of the hotel, Augusta tried in vain to wave down a National Guard truck. "It went right on by," he said, with some bitterness. "It went right on by."

More affirming was the saga of Dr. Joe Lasky, of which few people at Tulane were aware until after the Hurricane Katrina evacuation was over. But Lasky's journeys through New Orleans may have had a real impact on the evacuation – not so much at Tulane, but at Charity Hospital across Tulane Avenue.

Lasky, a pulmonary critical care specialist, was one of an estimated two hundred doctors at Tulane when New Orleans flooded. Under normal conditions he and the fellow members of his staff routinely rotated through several hospitals, including Tulane, Charity, the VA Medical Center, and Kindred Hospital. In advance of the storm the pulmonary critical care team saw to it that there was at least one physician and one physician-in-training at each facility.

Like everyone else at Tulane, Lasky went through an emotional roller coaster on Monday and Tuesday: anxiety as the hurricane hit, relief when the storm ended, and then confusion and fear when the flood waters rose. "After the hurricane came and went, it felt like it had been much ado about nothing," Lasky said. Starting early Tuesday morning, Lasky helped prioritize the order in which intensive care patients were evacuated.

Wednesday morning, with most of Tulane's serious patients evacuated, Lasky became restless and worried about how his team's patients were faring at other hospitals. He decided to check on them, but he had no way to call.

Without telling anyone, Lasky took his running shoes and a pair of dry socks, held them over his head, and waded out into the water. He made his way to St. Charles Avenue, where parts of the road were dry. He then put on his shoes and socks and went jogging through New Orleans in the direction of Kindred Hospital – three miles away. "I knew the route because I run it all the time," he later said. "But it was obviously a bit kooky I know. There were other people pushing shopping carts full of cigarette cartons down the road."

Incredibly, Lasky said he never felt threatened, even though New Orleans was under martial law and national news media were reporting that random gunfire was being heard all over the city. When asked if he was scared, he said, "I guess on a scale of one to ten, maybe it was a one. I guess there was some concern, but I don't think I was threatening anyone in my shorts and T-shirt and stethoscope."

Lasky found things in pretty good shape at Kindred Hospital. After staying there an hour, he ran over to his house in inner-city New Orleans. "I had to let Miss Clementine out," he said, referring to his coon hound. He then made his way back to Tulane. He didn't say anything to any of the hospital's administrators when he returned, figuring they wouldn't approve of his excursion.

The next day Lasky and physician Ross Klingsberg set out for Charity Hospital, this time in a canoe owned by an ambulance driver named Thomas (neither physician ever learned Thomas' last name). The situation there was not good. The doctors at Charity, a large, publicly owned hospital built during the era of Louisiana Governor Huey Long, had been told after the flood they would be evacuated by FEMA. But now, nearly sixty hours after the flood, there was still no sign of FEMA.

There were 340 patients at Charity, about fifty of them in critical condition. The intensive care unit there actually lost its central electrical system Monday at three a.m. due to a "ground fault" in one of the two emergency generators. For the rest of Monday Charity's staff provided electricity to the intensive care unit by running extension cords down hallways. When the flood came Monday night, the other emergency generator fixed to the building (located on the bottom floor) failed. From then on the only electrical power to be had at New Orleans' largest public hospital came from a series of portable generators. "We had our hands full," said Dr. Ben duBoisblanc, medical director of Charity's intensive care unit. "We were hand-bagging patients to keep people alive."

In spite of the conditions, duBoisblanc said, "People weren't panicking. They were doing what they always wanted to do, which is to stand by their patients in the greatest hour of need."

In fact, conditions were heavenly at Tulane compared to Charity.

One of the many people at Charity was a student nurse named Susan Sanborn. Interviewed months after the ordeal, Sanborn said that after electrical power went out everyone had to do a little bit of everything. "I was taking vital signs, trying to keep patients cool, feeding patients what little we had to feed them, running supplies, dealing with urine and feces," she said. Sanborn was one of many people who were hand-bagging patients in 30-minute shifts. "It requires more of a delicate touch than you might think," she said. "You had to be real careful about what you are doing because you have no way of monitoring what the patient's oxygen level was."

Throughout the Katrina ordeal, people at Tulane knew they were being protected by a team of loyal and heavily armed security guards. Charity's staff and physicians had no such assurance. Dr. Ruth Berggren, an infectious disease specialist at Charity, described her ordeal in an article for *The New England Journal of Medicine*. "I was never afraid of wind, water, fire, hunger, or disease," she wrote. "My moments of fear came when I was confronted by agitated, fearful human beings bearing firearms . . . The real Katrina disaster was not created by the elements but by a society whose fabric had been torn asunder by inequality, lack of education, and the inexplicable conviction that we should all have access to weapons that kill."

Like most of the people who worked at that hospital during the Katrina flood, Charity resident surgeon Jennifer McGee shrugged off many of the things she and others had to do to keep people alive. "We were focused on our patients," she said. "People were doing heroic things." However, in a lengthy interview after the ordeal, McGee admitted she and other staff members were constantly concerned about their safety. "If one of us had to go a long way, like from the fourth to the twelfth floor, we would travel in numbers," she said. "And at least one of us would carry a scalpel."

Charity Hospital was administratively linked to University

Hospital, which was located about three and half blocks away (not far on foot, but quite a long way after the flood waters rose). Dr. Dwayne Thomas, the CEO of Charity and University hospitals, was actually stationed at University Hospital after New Orleans flooded. On Tuesday Thomas sent word to the doctors at Charity Hospital that FEMA would evacuate them. "We were told we were going to be evacuated, but no one said how," duBoisblanc said a few weeks after the ordeal. "The message we were given was that FEMA and/or the National Guard would come in and assume complete control." In anticipation of this evacuation, the staff at Charity taped patients to spine boards and prepared medical records.

Tuesday came and went, and there was no sign of FEMA and no news from FEMA. Then, on Wednesday morning, the national media incorrectly reported that Charity Hospital had already been evacuated. "When we heard that, the reality of the situation sort of crystallized in my mind," said duBoisblanc. "We had a meeting and started formulating plans. And some of our residents and doctors got on the phone with CNN and told them that this report was wrong, that we were all still there." Among the physicians who participated in this public relations battle were two others who spent most of their time at Tulane after the flood, but who worked hard to help Charity: Lee Hamm, an internal medicine specialist and nephrologist, and Norm McSwain, a surgeon and the head of trauma at Charity. "We have been trying to call the mayor's office, we have been trying to call the governor's office…we have tried to use any inside pressure we can," McSwain was quoted as saying in an Associated Press story. "We are turning to you. Please help us."

Sometime on Wednesday Hamm hitched a canoe ride to Charity with two other physicians, Dr. Tyler Curiel and an orthopedic resident whose name Hamm later could not recall, to see how things were going there. The three men then paddled over to University Hospital, where Hamm spoke to Charity and University CEO Thomas. "I met with him very briefly," Hamm later said. "He told me Charity and University were supposed to have been evacuated that morning but it had never materialized, and that he didn't know what the plan of evacuation for them was at that time." Thomas also told Hamm he still thought Charity Hospital would be taken care of by the government. "He didn't ask anything of me," Hamm said. "He didn't ask me or Tulane for help. And he didn't ask me anything about what was taking place over at Tulane."[1]

That same day Charity evacuated four patients from the Saratoga garage. According to duBoisblanc it happened like this: After the national media corrected the erroneous story about Charity being already evacuated, a man who owned a helicopter company in Arkansas telephoned Charity and said he would send some helicopters to evacuate some of that hospital's more serious patients. Since Charity didn't have a helipad, and since the Charity staff could see the evacuation of Tulane proceeding across the street, Dr. Francesco Simeone at Charity asked the Arkansas company to send the helicopters to the top of the Tulane garage. A few hours later, using a truck of unknown origin, Charity moved four patients over to Tulane's garage. They were evacuated later that day.[2]

"Some of them left on military helicopters, which didn't have medics," duBoisblanc said. "Because of this, several of us had to go in the helicopters with the patients. They took us to a cloverleaf on the interstate. We put the patients in ambulances and took the helicopter back to Tulane and then managed to get over to Charity on a truck. I guess I got

---

[1] Numerous attempts to contact and interview Dwayne Thomas for this book were unsuccessful.

[2] According to officials in Tulane's command center, the Arkansas-based helicopters that duBoisblanc had referred to never arrived, and the Charity patients were evacuated by Acadian helicopters (at HCA's expense).

back to Charity at around one a.m. or so."

The next morning Charity's doctors talked about how to get the rest of their critical patients out. And this was about the time Lasky paddled over in his canoe.

Convinced that lives were dependent upon someone acting boldly, Lasky then canoed over to the massive refugee camp at the Superdome. Once there he located a convoy of trucks that had just delivered a shipment of water. Lasky went straight up to someone who seemed to be in charge and explained who he was and what needed to be done. "I pretty much just went up to random strangers, and I didn't have my scrubs and I didn't have my wallet and I didn't have my ID," he said. "All I had was a stethoscope and a flashlight."

Before long the entire convoy was on its way to Charity Hospital, although it didn't exactly take the direct route. "As strange as it sounds now, even those trucks couldn't talk to each other," he said. "I was in a convoy and we had to follow the truck in front of us and it first went to talk to the commander, and it was actually then that three trucks came with me to Charity.

"But I must say that the guys were great. The Louisiana National Guard were really great and cheerful and helpful."

It was in these three National Guard trucks that Charity Hospital loaded about half of its forty critical care patients on Thursday afternoon. They were then taken a couple of blocks away to the Tulane garage, where they were loaded onto pickup trucks and taken to the seventh floor of the garage to await evacuation by helicopter.

Another story of Tulane people wading out into the flood water is one Tulane and HCA officials regretted afterwards. On Wednesday morning a group of about twenty boats from the Louisiana Department of Wildlife and Fisheries pulled up to the ramp leading to the Saratoga Street Parking Garage and said they were there to evacuate patients to what they called an "evacuation center." They also passed on the news (which turned out to be inaccurate) that the air over the city of New Orleans was going to be declared a "no-fly zone" later that day because of sniper fire.

Tulane officials weren't sure what to do about this new opportunity. "We weren't going to just put someone on a boat and tell them we hoped things worked out for them," Lagarde said. So he first sent Jim Montgomery in one of the boats to see exactly where they were going. The Tulane CEO returned with news that the boats were evacuating people to a staging area along Interstate 10, where buses and ambulances were subsequently taking them to either Baton Rouge or Lafayette. "At that time, it seemed kind of along the same lines of what we were trying to do," Lagarde said. "So we decided to send the 'Superdome people' we had been caring for, along with some of our Tulane ambulatory patients, and later some of the family members of pediatric patients," who were anxious to leave Tulane so they could go be with their sick and injured children.

According to numerous interviews conducted months later, about eighty people left Tulane on these boats: two or three ambulatory Tulane patients, along with a couple of their family members; about eighteen family members of pediatric patients, and about thirty "Superdome people" and their family members. The "Superdome people" in serious condition stayed at Tulane and were later evacuated by helicopter directly to hospitals.

As it turned out, Tulane probably shouldn't have accepted the offer of help from the Department of Wildlife and Fisheries. One of the Tulane patients, a man named Timothy Gabriel, was taken to a military unit of some kind on dry land, where he and his wife waited for a few hours for an ambulance. He later ended up at Our Lady of the Lake Regional Medical Center in Baton Rouge.

The "Superdome people" apparently made it onto buses taking them to the Louis Armstrong Airport. When they left, Cheryl Turano, who had been watching them at the hospital, went with them in the function of caregiver and then came back to Tulane. "Every boat had the wildlife search and rescue man in the boat with you armed with guns," she said. "And I'll never forget going down Loyola Avenue, seeing people walking up to their necks in water, pulling floating tires with babies in them. I remember that all the stores were completely looted and destroyed. I remember that babies and children and adults were all standing on a dry spot just waiting to be rescued."

Turano said the boats were taken a few blocks down the street to a dry location, where the people from the Superdome were loaded in the back of civilian pickup trucks. "I think many of them were evacuated to the airport," she said. "The reason I think that is because I saw a couple of them at the airport a day or two later."

Meanwhile, in one of the most dramatic stories to emerge from the Tulane airlift, the parents of pediatric patients were taken four or five blocks away, then left in the heart of New Orleans. "We got to this dry area, and they told us there was a bus waiting for us on the other side of this building they were pointing at," said Tia Styles, whose six-year-old daughter, a cancer patient, had been evacuated by helicopter a few hours earlier. "So we walked around the building, and there wasn't anything there except a lot of water." The only people they could find were armed men who told the group they should go to the Superdome. "Well, we weren't going to go there!" said Robin Norwood, a parent who also left on the boats that day.

With the boats gone, the pediatric parents argued amongst themselves about what to do next. Some said they should go back to Tulane, but the water was very deep in that direction. Some said they should head where the water appeared shallower. Meanwhile there were three things the group didn't have that it needed badly: a gun (New Orleans was under martial law by this time); a map (no one among them knew anything about the city); and an operable cell phone.

After a leader emerged, the group started walking, first on dry land, then in ankle deep water, and eventually into knee-deep water. They walked in a southeast direction, anywhere from six to twelve blocks, depending on whose account is the most accurate. At the corner of Poydras and Carondelet streets – just west of the French Quarter – they ran across a crew from Fox News Channel. "I saw them emerging from the water en masse, all of them wearing green scrubs," reporter Jeff Goldblatt later said. "It was surreal."

Members of the group told Goldblatt who they were and what had happened to them. "I knew I wanted to help them, but I didn't know what to do," he said. "I mean, there were a lot of desperate people hanging out on this corner, because of a rumor that buses would come there. I couldn't let on that I was helping anyone because I was afraid I'd be mobbed with others wanting help. Meanwhile I had a job to do and couldn't be gone for very long. I was broadcasting just about every hour from that location."

Goldblatt told a member of the Tulane group, Sue Roesky, to come with him, leaving the others there temporarily. He took Roesky to the W New Orleans Hotel (where he was staying) and asked hotel manager Marcus Reinders if the people he had discovered could be sheltered in the hotel. Reinders went a step further, saying they could ride on some chartered buses that were about to take hotel guests to a public shelter in Lafayette. "My original thought was that these people could seek shelter here, but when I met them and they told me they need to get to their children, we offered them space on these buses," Reinders said.

Goldblatt and Roesky then went back to fetch the rest of the group. "They came back and didn't tell us anything about where we were going," Styles later remembered. "They told us to walk in small groups and not say anything to anyone. You see, they didn't want anyone else to know we had a way out, because everyone would want to take it."

The pediatric parents made it to the W Hotel, and to the bus, and to the Lafayette shelter, and eventually to Texas Children's Hospital, where they were reunited with their children. They were obviously grateful to reporter Jeff Goldblatt for helping them in their hour of need. "He saved our lives," Roesky said.

Tulane officials were notably upset when they learned what had happened to the pediatric parents they had sent by boat with the Department of Wildlife and Fisheries. "We obviously never ever would have put anyone on those boats if we had any idea that anything like that could have taken place," Jim Montgomery said.

Chapter Nine
The View from the Air

There were many heroes in the Tulane airlift. Among them were those who flew helicopters and those who served as crew members of helicopters. "After what we went through, I have an incredible amount of respect for pilots," said Mel Lagarde. "They can fly and land those damned things anywhere."

In researching this book, several people who flew missions on behalf of Tulane were interviewed. Here are some of their stories:

Dan Bitton normally flies for a Chicago-area police department. As mentioned earlier, he flew his EC-135 south on Tuesday night and, after unloading gear in Lafayette, set out for Tulane at about eight p.m.

"Flying into New Orleans was one of the most dangerous things I've ever done in fifteen thousand hours of flying," said Bitton, whose appearance and accent led more than one person to compare him to

Rambo, the Sylvester Stallone character. "I'd never flown over New Orleans before, and there I was, at low elevation over the city in pitch-black darkness, trying to find a parking garage. And it was dark, believe me. All I had was the latitude and a longitude of the hospital, but not the parking garage. That's what made the first flight interesting."

Bitton wore night-vision goggles, which he said took some getting used to. "The goggles work pretty well as far as seeing through the darkness. But you have to constantly transition from using them to not using them. So you're looking underneath the goggles to the instruments and then back through the goggles to see outside. And when you first look up again you see blackness until you reacquire the goggles."

Since Bitton was such a seasoned pilot, one would assume he had plenty of experience with night-vision equipment. Instead he said he "had just learned how to use those goggles." As far as landings were concerned, "I recently went through refresher training, and told the instructor I wanted to do dark landings in a confined area of the Wisconsin woods. He told me I was absolutely nuts. He said all the other guys wanted to get out of some of this stuff, but I wanted to do it. And I told him he was right, but I wanted to know how to do it just in case I had an emergency. So we did it about fifteen times. The first twelve or thirteen scared me to death and the last two or three scared me, but not that much. Had I not done that, I would not have been able to land at Tulane that night."

Bitton logged sixty flight hours in four and a half days in New Orleans. "Let's face it: you throw all the normal regulations about flight hours out the window at a time like that," he said. "But by the same token, we didn't do anything that two hundred other pilots didn't do."

When asked about logistical problems in New Orleans, Bitton immediately mentioned the difficulty in obtaining fuel, which often required a one- to two-hour wait. "That was really frustrating," he said. "Finally, I just told this guy who was refueling at the airport that I was commandeering some fuel because he was being difficult. I can do that as a law enforcement officer in an emergency situation."

Bitton said one thing that made the project easier was the support HCA showed. "The people there were great. I remember at one point we landed in Lafayette at about 3:30 in the morning and one of the executives with Southwest Medical Center was there making us cheese and bologna sandwiches. They were just very appreciative, very supportive. And they were so much farther ahead than any other organization down there that it was just amazing. I've spoken to several groups since my experience, and I've told everyone that HCA is a role model for how they reacted to that disaster."

Greg Miller is a pilot for St. Louis Helicopter, flying an S-58 Sikorsky aircraft. The day after the flood he was en route to New Orleans carrying equipment to a food warehouse when he was told over the radio that, after that mission, he should proceed to Lakeview Medical Center in Covington. By Thursday afternoon he had joined the Tulane airlift, flying an estimated twenty sorties (or round trips) – so many, in fact, that Miller's aircraft stood out in the memory of HCA's Mel Lagarde. "We'd put eight people in that helicopter and they would take off, and before I knew it they'd be back landing again," Lagarde said later.

Asked months later about the experience of flying in relief of the Katrina flood, Miller said the potential for air-to-air collisions was very clear. "There was a big trapezoid-shaped flight area over the entire city of New Orleans, and to fly into that area you had to check in with an EP-3 aircraft that was kind of running the show and tell him what code you were squawking and what your destination was," said Miller. "But once you were in that area you were on your own. There was no flight following. And believe me, there was every helicopter known to man flying over that city. The word for it was chaos."

Miller said altitude clearance was a must. "There were several times where we would be flying over the flooded area and we would look down and there would be a helo hoisting someone off a roof that you couldn't see until you got right on top of them. Because of this we'd try to stay at or above five hundred feet whenever possible to get clearance over those rescue helicopters."

There were so many other helicopters in the air, in fact, that Miller changed the normal configuration of his crew. "I had a crew of two along with myself – a crew chief and a second," he said. "Normally they ride in the back. But there were so many helos out there that I needed one of them up front with me to help me look around. The other crew member would control entry and egress from the helicopter and make sure everyone was seated and we weren't exceeding our weight limits and such."

Miller said he didn't fly at night more than necessary. "Like most of the other civilian operators, I don't have NVG [night-vision goggles] capability or anything like that. I mean, it was like flying into a black hole because the whole city was dark. And I can tell you that flying over Lake Pontchartrain when the causeway isn't lit up is no fun because there is no reference to guide you."

Miller was asked what images of the rescue will stick with him, and he began describing scenes of despair and gratitude.

The things we saw on top of the garage were really something. I remember looking out and seeing people walking out in scrubs and slippers or whatever, carrying stuff in a sheet or a pillowcase or backpack. They were in various states of dress and condition, and in expression they looked like deer in the headlights for the most part.

They would look up at me in the cockpit and try to get my attention and mouth the words 'Thank you.' I saw that I don't know how many times. Meanwhile the loading process would be stopped over and over again because people would hug my crewmen and not let go. One time a huge gentleman who must have weighed three or four hundred pounds came out of a wheelchair and gave my crewman a big bear hug. And he just would not let go.

An emergency medical technician supervisor for HCA's Medical City Children's Hospital in Dallas, Tim Beasley and his colleagues left for Lafayette on Tuesday night with about seven hundred pounds of baby food, formula, diapers, and water. "At first they wanted my team to stay there and help them care for all the patients they were getting inundated with from all over New Orleans," he said. "But our team specializes in neonatal intensive care and pediatric intensive care patients. So they decided to send us in."

Tulane's babies and children had already been evacuated by this time. On Wednesday morning Beasley flew on board an Acadian Ambulance helicopter to Touro Infirmary, located across New Orleans. "They needed us to get seven premature babies," Beasley said.

As soon as the helicopter landed at Touro, nurses came running out to it. "You could tell they were anxious to get them out of there," Beasley said. Beasley hadn't considered the idea that they might have to carry all seven babies on one flight, but he suddenly realized they would have to do just that. "Now, I wasn't sure how we were going to get those seven babies out of there because we wouldn't normally consider doing such a thing. So I took two stretchers and put little nursery cribs on them. I then wrapped the babies all snug and put three in each container and then carried the seventh one all the way back."

Beasley said the babies were so small, and their medical records so large, that the records were much heavier than the babies. "I mean, these are premature babies, and so they are really tiny. But each of them had a big thick medical record with them. So I was loading what looked like seven big desk Bibles in the back."

Beasley was concerned about how much noise seven babies would make on the flight back. That, it turned out, wasn't a problem. "None of the babies were sedated, but luckily only one baby cried on the flight," he said. "I guess the drone and vibration of the helicopter helped put them to sleep."

The helicopter landed in Lafayette, where the seven babies were transferred to fixed-wing planes and taken to Dallas. Four of them were treated at HCA's Medical City Children's Hospital, three transferred to Presbyterian Hospital of Dallas.

That same morning Cheryl Friday, a neonatal intensive care nurse at Women's and Children's Hospital, and Colby Johnson, a respiratory therapist at that same hospital, flew to Touro on a similar mission. When the Acadian helicopter lifted off on its return flight, it carried six infants. "We had two in a crib, arranged head to toe," Friday later said, "and Colby and I were each carrying two in these special evacuation gowns we were wearing.

"These gowns are actually designed for just such an emergency, with six pockets in the front and six in the back, each of them big enough to carry a baby in. I've been a nurse for twenty-eight years, and I've never even opened one of those gowns up, let alone used one."

Friday said that, given the situation, the flight and the transfer of the infants went as smoothly as possible. "The babies were all wrapped up with their identifications with them and their medical records all ready, and there was no chance of us getting them mixed up or anything," she said. "Touro had done a very good job getting ready."

Chuck Brainerd was the owner of Firehawk Helicopters Inc., a Leesburg, Florida, based firm with six aircraft (five of which are Blackhawks, which carry up to eighteen people). When Katrina slammed into the Gulf Coast, he assumed his company would immediately be hired by the federal government to fly relief missions. (Firehawk's main line of work is fighting fires for the USDA Forest Service.) But in the days following Katrina, the government didn't call.

"Finally, on Wednesday night, I told my wife we were going in on our own nickel if we had to in order to help those people in New Orleans. So the next day I left. Then, on a fuel stop in Mobile, Alabama, I was told that Chuck Hall of HCA had called."

Like the other pilots, Brainerd emphasized just how concerned he was about running into another helicopter. "Once you left the New Orleans airport, the main concern was to try not to have a midair collision," he said. "We would be hovering and waiting to land on the rooftop and some helo would take off and another would jump in front of us and land. And then we'd head back to the airport and there might be thirty or thirty-five helos on the ramp at one time. It was kind of a mess."

Many of the people at Tulane, in weeks following the flood, said the airlift was "shut down" on Thursday night because of gunfire. Brainerd said this wasn't the case. "It wasn't that we were told not to fly," he said. "We just needed some rest. So we went back to the Fixed Base Operation, which is sort of the gas station for airplanes. We ate some Chef Boyardee that someone had left there, and we got some sleep in this office."

In fact, Brainerd said he was far more concerned about midair collisions than he was about gunfire. "Obviously no one likes it, but we weren't going to shut down any missions for it. We figured it was just sporadic pistol fire or something; we weren't that worried about it. I don't think we ever got shot at. But I must say the whole experience was like working in a war zone. You didn't even get the feeling you were in America when we were doing this."

Like Miller, Brainerd said he was impressed with the care and concern that Tulane's people showed. "They carried patients on stretchers and when the stretchers ran out they had people on folding tables with IVs stuck in them," he said. "Whatever had to be done, whatever could be done, they did it. The situation called for breaking the rules."

And like Miller, Brainerd said the passengers on his helicopters did not restrain their happiness when they were lifted off the roof of the garage. "Usually they would be real quiet until we took off. Then, after we lifted off and cleared that hotel next to the parking garage, everyone would give a shout for joy."

The Tulane airlift was arranged and carried out with such haste that few of the pilots involved had a chance to meet each other. But one old acquaintance was renewed.

In 1982 Chuck Brainerd was a member of the Florida National Guard, scheduled to go on summer duty, when his wife went into labor. He called his unit for permission to stay at home for the birth of his son. It was granted by his unit's operations officer – a man named John Holland.

During the Tulane airlift Brainerd flew his Blackhawk helicopter for about six sorties on Thursday and ten on Friday. Brainerd's copilot – the person John Holland was exchanging notes with on the roof of the Tulane parking garage – was Brainerd's son. Holland didn't know this until two weeks later.

"I called him after all this was over," Brainerd said. "We were talking about old times. And then I said, do you remember that baby you gave me permission to stay home for? Well, that baby was the twenty-three-year-old copilot with me at Tulane!"

Mel Lagarde, Jim Montgomery, and Mike Kiernan
Photo courtesy of HCA

Sharif Omar *Photo courtesy of HCA*

George Jamison *Photo courtesy of Bill Carey*

Jeanne James, Danita Sullivan, and Kim Ryan
serve dinner on Sunday night.
Photo courtesy of Marta Rozans

Kim Ryan and daughter Cheryl Turano
Photo courtesy of Bill Carey

John Holland *Photo courtesy of HCA*

A man unwisely crosses the street in front of Tulane Hospital during Hurricane Katrina.
Photo courtesy of Norm McSwain

Water inundates the floor of the Tulane Hospital lobby.
Photo courtesy of Norm McSwain

A canoe docked in front of Tulane's emergency room
Photo courtesy of Norm McSwain

The Tulane sign damaged during the storm
Photo courtesy of HCA

Photo courtesy of Marta Rozans

Photo courtesy of HCA

Photo courtesy of HCA

Photo courtesy of HCA

Photo courtesy of HCA

Views from Tulane after the flood

Photo courtesy of HCA

Photo courtesy of Norm McSwain

Photo courtesy of HCA

Photo courtesy of HCA

Photo courtesy of Norm McSwain

Brandy Schaaf looks at her two-week-old daughter Drew – one of the first babies evacuated during the Tulane airlift.

Photo courtesy of Steve Schaaf

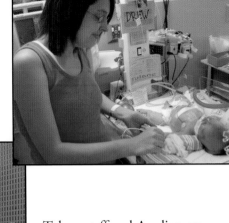

Tulane staff and Acadian crew members load infant Drew Schaaf onto a helicopter.

Photo courtesy of Steve Schaaf

Another patient is evacuated.

Photo courtesy of Norm McSwain

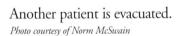

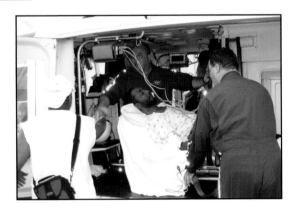

John Latino, husband of a Tulane employee, rests between trips up and down the garage with patients in the back of his truck.

Photo courtesy of Marta Rozans

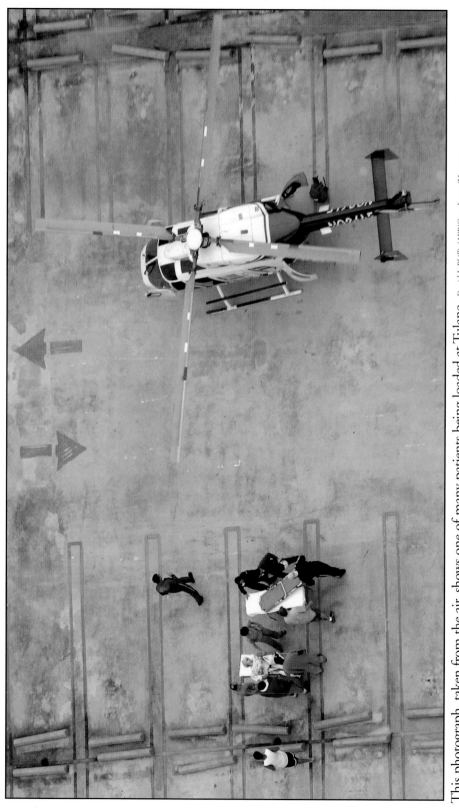

This photograph, taken from the air, shows one of many patients being loaded at Tulane. *David J. Phillip/AFP/Getty Images/Newscom*

Some of the many helicopters that came and went during the Katrina airlift

All photos courtesy of HCA

Some of the "Superdome people"
Photo courtesy of Marta Rozans

Boats from the Louisiana
Fish and Wildlife Agency
load people from Tulane.
Photo courtesy of HCA

A meeting of doctors at
Charity Hospital
Photo courtesy of Norm McSwain

The Tulane Command
Center on Wednesday,
after the power went out
Photo courtesy of Norm McSwain

While Mel Lagarde and Jim Montgomery deal with an increasingly tense situation on Thursday, a CNN photographer stands behind them.

Photo courtesy of HCA

Tulane nurse Jennifer Brocato-Diecidue, in the foreground, hand bags a Charity patient at the Tulane garage on Thursday.

Photo courtesy of Marta Rozans

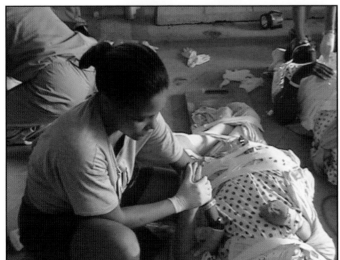

Tulane nurse Nicole Henry-Hammons holds the hand of a Charity patient awaiting departure.

Photo courtesy of HCA

Tulane security personnel were ubiquitous during the airlift. *Photo courtesy of HCA*

HAM radio operators try to get things working. *Photo courtesy of HCA*

Montgomery smiles while people board a CH-47.

Photo courtesy of Norm McSwain

HCA Chief Operating Officer Richard Bracken *Photo courtesy of HCA*

Chuck Hall, head of HCA's North Florida division *Photo courtesy of HCA*

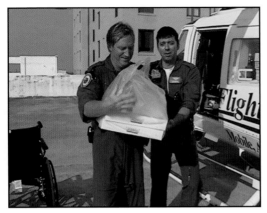

Pilots unload doughnuts.
Photo courtesy of HCA

The explosion east of New Orleans early
Friday morning
Photo by Norm McSwain

Marta, Micky, and Sam Rozans
Photo courtesy of Marta Rozans

Tulane surgeon Stephen Gale sleeps on
the garage with his young son.
Photo courtesy of HCA

Marine Sergeant Kraft   *Photo by Norm McSwain*

People queue up for hours
and hours waiting for a
spot on a helicopter.

Photos courtesy of HCA

Hospital officials lead a line
of people across the top
floor of the Saratoga garage,
where they will board a
helicopter.

Photo courtesy of HCA

With the arrival of
Chinooks, the pace of the
airlift greatly increased.

Photo courtesy of Norm McSwain

Photo courtesy of HCA

Tulane staff and family members await evacuation from the airport.

Photo courtesy of Marta Rozans

Helicopters landing and taking off at the airport *Photo courtesy of HCA*

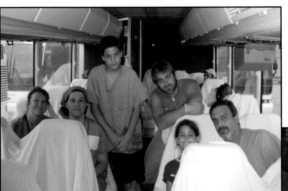

Kim Bell, Hope Latino, Michael Latino (standing), Lucas Richmond, Theresa Latino, and John Latino on the bus ride to Lafayette *Photo courtesy of Dominic Latino*

Theresa Latino in one of the Lafayette shelters set up by HCA employees in that city
Photo courtesy of Hope Latino

Starting in late September, HCA financed a complete cleanup
of the Tulane Hospital building. *Photos courtesy of Bill Carey*

Ricky Ezell, Warren Breaux, and Robby McDowell carry the American flag that had hung from the Tulane Hospital building during the Katrina airlift. *Lee Celano/Reuters/Newscom*

Tulane employees lower the flag.
Photo courtesy of Bill Carey

Mel Lagarde watches the flag lowered over the side of the Tulane Hospital building.
Photo courtesy of Bill Carey

People who were involved in the Tulane evacuation pose on the day the hospital reopened. From left to right: Kim Ryan, Mel Lagarde, Stiles Clarke, Sharif Omar, Bryan Dean, Kim Graham, John Holland, Danita Sullivan, Lee Hamm, and Mike Kiernan. *Photo courtesy of Bill Carey*

Montgomery speaks at the reopening ceremony at Tulane. *Photo courtesy of Bill Carey*

HCA chief executive officer Jack Bovender presents nurse Christina Riviere with a photo of herself carrying an infant out of a helicopter in Alexandria, Louisiana. *Photo courtesy of Bill Carey*

Chapter Ten
Rescue from the Airport

Nearly everyone at Tulane – including patients' family members, Tulane staff, and family members of Tulane staff – eventually took part in the remarkable airlift begun on Tuesday, August 30, 2005. But the magnitude of the air evacuation wasn't decided upon immediately. Tulane officials were being told continually that FEMA or the Louisiana National Guard or some other government-related entity was poised to rescue everyone and restore order to the city. So was every other hospital in New Orleans. Unlike many other hospitals, however, HCA operated under the assumption that government help would not arrive in time. "We knew there was a chance the cavalry would show up," said HCA chief executive officer Jack Bovender. "But we decided on Tuesday morning we were going to take responsibility for this ourselves and assume the worst. We were going to assume that no one was going to come to our rescue."

Meanwhile the idea that most people at Tulane would leave by some means other than helicopter remained very much in place throughout Tuesday afternoon, Tuesday night, and even Wednesday morning. A land evacuation would have posed difficult logistical problems – most notably, the fact that the hospital was surrounded by water on all sides. But it was theoretically possible. After all, it was possible to get vehicles into New Orleans and very close to Tulane (that is, if National Guard roadblocks let them through). The depth of the water varied greatly from block to block, dependent on the subtle slopes of the city (which is why the New Orleans Public Library, just across the street from Tulane Hospital, sustained very little damage as a result of the flood). If the vehicles were high enough off the ground – and big National Guard trucks were – they could drive right up to Tulane's front door.

And while the dramatic events at Tulane were playing out, HCA quietly orchestrated successful and safe evacuations of patients, staff, and family members from DePaul-Tulane Behavioral Health Center, in another part of New Orleans, and Lakeside Hospital, in the New Orleans suburb of Metairie. Those facilities weren't surrounded by water like Tulane was. But those evacuations also posed logistical challenges, which HCA had managed to overcome.

There were, for instance, nearly a hundred people at DePaul – about forty of them psychiatric patients. When the storm hit, director of clinical services Evelyn Nolting was in charge. Later she emphasized how difficult it was to remain calm with flood waters rising in other parts of New Orleans. "We were never engulfed by water," she said. "But there was always the fear that we, too, were going to be."

Communications were bad on Monday and Tuesday. Finally, on Wednesday morning, she found an operable phone. "I called a 1-800 number that I knew reached HCA's information systems office," she said. "Once I got someone, I told the person at the other end of the line who I was and how he needed to help us." The message eventually reached Sam Hazen, who arranged to have Alan Fabian, COO of Southwest Medical Center in Lafayette, flown in by helicopter and to have two buses sent to DePaul (one of which HCA rented from a Lafayette bowling alley). There was considerable drama when only one of the buses arrived at 6:30 that evening. "For a while it looked like we were going to have to decide who would go and who would stay," Nolting said. But when the other one showed up an hour later, the staff, patients, and family members made it out.

Metairie's Lakeside Hospital had thirty-four patients and about 250 staff and family members when the storm hit. In the immediate wake of the hurricane, the service road leading to the hospital campus was flooded from storm surge. That water slowly subsided on Monday night. But on Tuesday morning, with news of the situation in New Orleans coming in, the staff had to deal with unexpected panic. "There was this rumor going around that levees near us were going to be intentionally breached to offset the flooding into New Orleans," said COO Andre duPlessis, the senior ranking official at Lakeside.

"This made no sense at all to me, and I didn't believe it. But people did. And they were scurrying around getting their belongings packed, asking me how they were going to get them out of there. It was as if someone had gotten on the loudspeaker and said that the floodwaters were coming."

Lakeside had plenty of food, water, electricity, fuel, and excellent communications with HCA. "We could have gone five days without having to replenish," duPlessis said. But because of the situation in nearby New Orleans, the decision was made to evacuate the hospital. On Tuesday and early Wednesday, the staff discharged some of its patients, and evacuated the rest by helicopter. Among them were a dozen neonatal intensive care patients, flown to Women's and Children's Hospital in Lafayette, and about half a dozen adults, airlifted to HCA's Dauterive Hospital in New Iberia, Louisiana. The staff and family members left by personal vehicle, and Lakeside was evacuated by Wednesday night.

What eventually doomed the notion of a land rescue of Tulane wasn't geography and the flood so much as it was the situation in New Orleans. Unlike DePaul and Lakeside, Tulane was located downtown, only blocks away from the Superdome. This fact weighed heavily in the minds of HCA officials as they abandoned the idea of evacuating everyone by motor vehicle. "We had in the board room here a TV with either Fox News or CNN on it all the time," Jack Bovender said. "We could see the images of the disaster at the Superdome; images of buses showing up and getting mobbed; images of people being taken off in boats and then left alone on interstate overpasses."

The media may have painted a picture of New Orleans that was worse than reality. But there was, in fact, widespread looting, and occasional gunfire could be heard in the city. "We could see looting from where we were," said deputy chief of security Warren Breaux. "In fact, the looting started after the storm and before the flood. They hit the Walgreens down the street and the Hospital Drug Store across the street. That much we could see.

"And then after the water came up we could see all sorts of things. I remember at one point we saw three youngsters coming down, with one in a big motorboat and two pushing the boat. I assumed they were stealing it."

Considering this situation, the decision was made on Wednesday to evacuate everyone by helicopter. "Mel [Lagarde] was talking about ground transportation, and we just said to him, 'It's becoming a jungle out there and we just can't do that,'" Bovender said.

Helicopters aren't cheap, and, as the evacuation developed, HCA assumed it would be stuck with the tab for these evacuation costs. "Yes, it is expensive to fly everyone out by helicopter," Bovender said. "But as we went though this process, there never was a thought about how much this would cost. We were operating under the old military axiom that says

'Leave no one behind.' We were not going to lose these patients. We weren't going to lose these staff members. We weren't even going to lose a dog or cat."

With this decision made, HCA began looking for larger aircraft to take part in the air evacuation. To this end, late on Wednesday afternoon, HCA hired Firehawk Helicopters, a Leesburg-based firm that owned several civilian Blackhawk helicopters. When extraneous equipment is removed from their interior, Firehawk's helicopters can carry up to twenty people.

Since hospital officials do not necessarily have advanced knowledge in parking garage design and helicopter weight specifications, there was at first some concern about whether the Saratoga Street Parking Garage could hold a Blackhawk. At this point reassurance came from an unexpected source. Brad Smith was a Blackhawk pilot for the Louisiana National Guard and the father of an eighteen-year-old patient at Tulane who had undergone brain surgery three days before the hurricane. Sometime on Tuesday hospital officials invited family members wanting to volunteer for odd jobs to come to a short meeting. At that meeting Smith heard Tulane CEO Jim Montgomery speculating as to whether the garage would be strong enough to hold a large helicopter. Smith stepped in and assured him it would. "A Blackhawk weighs as little as fifteen thousand pounds and as much as twenty-two thousand pounds, depending on whether it is loaded down," he later said. "Meanwhile a garage is built to hold a hundred cars per level, each of which might weigh five thousand pounds. It'll easily hold it."

The addition of Blackhawks gave HCA's corporate office a sense of confidence that it really could pull off such a large airlift. But this still left the question of where everyone would be taken. Knowing where HCA's hospitals were located, and which ones had sustained damage during the storm, the decision was quickly made to take the staff and family members to Lafayette, where HCA had two hospitals (Southwest Medical

Center and Women's and Children's Hospital). Personnel at those facilities, who were already taking care of patients being evacuated from Tulane and other New Orleans hospitals, began making arrangements to care for, feed, and shelter more than a thousand evacuees.

Meanwhile the idea of creating an intermediate destination – where helicopters could land and drop off passengers who could then be transferred to buses – first came to Mel Lagarde and Sam Hazen on Tuesday night. "It just dawned on me that flying all the helicopters directly to another hospital was going to take too long," Lagarde said. "And we were being told by pilots that Interstate 10 was clear and that the town was dry west of the airport."

As it happened, Lagarde was on the New Orleans aviation board. It took him a couple of phone calls to administratively clear the idea of HCA creating a staging area at the airport.

So now HCA had a plan, but not an easy one. The more the people at HCA thought about it, the more it became obvious that Tulane needed to send a person, or people, to both Lafayette and the New Orleans airport to help organize the effort. After all, there was no telling what the situation was at the airport. And there were things that might not occur to people in Lafayette as they planned to deal with Tulane's evacuees.

Picking people for both of these jobs was a split-second decision. Lagarde decided to send Karen Troyer-Caraway, whose corporate title was vice president of business development, to Lafayette. "Communications had become a real problem by this time," she later said. "The main idea of sending me to Lafayette was to bring everyone up there up to speed on what they needed to do to get ready for all the people we were sending." There were many reasons Lagarde picked Troyer-Caraway, not the least of which was that her husband was a police officer with the Kenner,

Louisiana, police department. "Kenner is where the airport was," she explained, "and we had already heard that getting buses into the airport was not going to be easy." Troyer-Caraway left the Tulane garage at about two p.m. on Wednesday, flying on an aircraft that also took ambulatory patients.

A few hours later Lagarde told COO Kim Ryan to get on the next helicopter heading for the airport. "I told Mel I wouldn't go without my daughter," Ryan said. "He said 'fine,' and I found Cheryl. We didn't have time to grab anything; we just jumped on the next helicopter and got out."

When Ryan and Turano walked into the terminal, they were shocked at what they saw. Patients from just about every hospital in New Orleans (other than Tulane) had been evacuated to the airport, and the terminal looked like a large military hospital shortly after a battle. Military units had set up tents inside the building in an attempt to keep critical patients away from less serious ones. But the vast majority of people were still strewn about. "There were patients on the floor just about everywhere you looked, in every nook and cranny of the airport," Turano later said. "When you walked through them, they would just grab you and pull at you and cry for help."

Turano vividly remembered her first, and only, visit to one of the airport's bathrooms, which were popular destinations because the airport actually had running water. "There must have been twenty naked women in that little bathroom using the water and just throwing it all over their bodies and using the hand sanitizer and just rubbing it everywhere."

The situation at the Louis Armstrong Airport was shocking. Months after Katrina, airport operations manager Rich Cutillo said the employees there did the best they could given the conditions. "We are an airport, and when it comes to emergencies, the thing we are generally prepared to deal with is a plane crash, where you might have three or four hundred people involved," he said. "Well, during the few days following the flood, thirty thousand people descended on this place, many of them in great need. And most of them had no way to get out of here once they got here.

"It was chaos, and we honestly had a handful of employees here because we hadn't expected any such thing. And I can tell you that in spite of the situation here, we had some people doing some incredibly good things. We are, for instance, very proud of the fact that we had seven thousand flights in and out of here during the few days after Katrina. It was like the Saigon airlift. But we had no accidents."

After arriving, Ryan and Turano located aviation director Roy Williams, who helped them find an out-of-the-way place outside the airport to stage their operations the next day. Since they needed a way to cordon off their area, they tracked down several dozen chairs.

By this time it was late on Wednesday night, and sometime during that evening arrangements had been made to ferry Ryan and Turano to the nearby home of Karen Troyer-Caraway to spend the night. Troyer-Caraway's husband, a police officer, drove to the airport, somehow located Ryan and Turano, and took them to his home. He wasn't too happy about this, however, because he knew something his wife didn't know — that their home wasn't a safe or comfortable place to be at that point. "He dropped us off and went back to work," Ryan said. "And things weren't too good there. There was no running water and no power and the neighborhood was completely abandoned.

"We got to sleep on a bed. But that's about all I can say about it."

A hundred miles away, in Lafayette, Troyer-Caraway was quite busy. "There was a lot to be done in terms of coordinating what kinds of supplies we needed to put on the buses," she said. "So I stayed up all night."

HCA had ordered twenty buses, which were en route from

Houston to Lafayette by that time. Some of the things the company had decided to put on the buses would have been easy to predict, such as bottled water and snack food. But one thing that wasn't as obvious was surgical slippers – more than a thousand pairs of them.

"We decided that the first part of the decontamination process was to make everyone take off their shoes and socks, throw them away, and wipe off their feet with baby wipes," Troyer-Caraway said. "Because even though the water was only on the first floor of the hospital, there had been people walking through it and then back into the hospital. So by this time the carpets all over the Tulane Hospital building were inundated with this water, and we didn't know exactly what was in it. But of course we knew there was raw sewage and some dead bodies floating around New Orleans."

Troyer-Caraway was amazed at how uncomfortably cold she got sitting in the air-conditioned Women's and Children's Hospital. "I was so used to the incredible heat of Tulane Hospital that I was freezing up there," she said. "So Leona [Boullion] wrapped me in a blanket, and I stayed in that blanket all night." Largely because of Troyer-Caraway's reaction to the air conditioning, HCA packed hundreds of blankets for the journey to New Orleans.

Then came the bus ride from Lafayette to the Louis Armstrong Airport – a story in itself. The buses arrived from Houston on time, and they left Lafayette at 5:30 Thursday morning. After a stop in Gonzalez, Louisiana, to pick up more police officers, they headed for New Orleans, by this time accompanied by about a dozen police cars and carrying about twenty nurses and HCA volunteers. In spite of how prepared they might have appeared, no one was sure they would make it. "We didn't know what we would encounter," Troyer-Caraway said. "I spoke to my husband in the middle of the night, and he told me he didn't think there was any way we would get where we were going because the National Guard controlled the airport."

When they arrived in Kenner, the buses took a back way into the airport, working their way past fallen trees and power lines. The convoy made it to a place across the runway from the main terminal, in an area reserved for general aviation and refueling, but was then told it couldn't proceed to the terminal. For a while all looked lost. Then they saw a white pickup truck with an airport logo on the side of it — a vehicle being driven by an airport operations supervisor named Bob Loup. "I knocked on his window and I introduced myself and told him who I was and what my problem was," Troyer-Caraway said. "And I told him I was coordinating all of this with the FEMA office out of Gonzales," which wasn't exactly true.

"In any case, he told me to jump in the truck and tell the buses to follow him. And that's just what happened. So we led twenty buses and fifteen police cars over two active taxiways and a runway over to the Federal Express terminal and then from there to the Delta terminal." Loup thus became one of the many people unassociated with HCA who played a key role in the successful and safe evacuation of Tulane Hospital. "He helped us shuttle buses all day," she said. "I don't know how we could have done it without him."

Loup, who left the airport to work as a real estate appraiser after Katrina, said he remembered helping with the Tulane evacuation. "On that day everyone who worked at the airport was everywhere, and no one knew anything," Loup said. "I was driving around just looking to see if I could find something I could do to help.

"I ran into Karen, and she told me who she was and what she needed. And I told her to get in. I decided that if there was something I could do to help someone get through this, then I was going to do it."

Kim Ryan and Cheryl Turano were, by this time, back at the airport. When the buses arrived, everyone worked together to prepare the staging area. But then, as helicopters arrived on the nearby tarmac, the HCA people who were there to help realized their job would be an awkward one. After all, this wasn't just where people from Tulane were being evacuated; there were helicopters flying in from all over the New Orleans area. And there weren't nearly enough people at the airport to greet, direct, and assist the thousands of refugees who were coming in from all corners of the city. "These pilots were in such a big hurry to get people out of New Orleans that they would often land, help their passengers get off the helicopter, and then take off and leave them there on the hot pavement with no instructions on where to go," Ryan said. "And often these were hospital patients, or elderly people, or whatever. So by default it became our job to greet these people and direct them into the airport terminal unless they had a green wristband, which meant they were one of ours."

Since the HCA people were aware of conditions inside the airport, this wasn't an easy thing to do. "I must admit that this really made us feel awful," said Turano. "Here were all these people, hundreds and thousands of them, and they would get off the plane and say 'thank you' and hug you and everything. And they looked happy to be there, in spite of the fact that they had no shoes and some of them weren't dressed and they looked so awful. But they had no idea what they were walking into when they were walking into that airport. It was scary in there, and it was getting worse.

"We felt horrible that we were sending them in there. But there was nothing else we could do."

As helicopters began to arrive from Tulane, people disembarking from them began to "decontaminate," as directed. As had been planned, employees and family members coming off the helicopters that day took off their shoes and socks and tossed them into big red trash bags, never to be seen again. After ditching their footwear, everyone cleaned their feet thoroughly with baby wipes; put on a pair of surgical slippers; and took a bottle of water and a granola bar. Eventually, when enough bodies had accumulated, they were loaded onto a bus and set to Lafayette.

Chapter Eleven
Big Birds

All things considered, the airport staging area worked well and dramatically increased the pace of the airlift. But there was one problem: things weren't moving fast enough. It wasn't that the pilots weren't working hard enough, or that there weren't enough of them. The problem was that the helicopters were too small. "Pretty much all of them on Thursday were helicopters that carried four or six people," said Kim Ryan. Meanwhile the hundreds of people left at Tulane were beginning to wonder just how long this operation would continue. "At times it felt like we were trying to empty a swimming pool one bucketful of water at a time," one Tulane official said.

This in mind, it's time to shift the focus of the story from the staging area at the Louis Armstrong Airport back to some of the other places in which this saga was taking place: the roof of the Tulane garage; HCA's corporate offices in Tallahassee and Nashville; the Louisiana Superdome; and even the office of Louisiana Governor Kathleen Blanco.

Like many parts of the Tulane airlift, this part of the story isn't entirely coherent. But it's extremely important. What we know for certain is that late Thursday afternoon, National Guard CH-47 Chinook helicopters began taking part in the Tulane airlift. Unlike the civilian helicopter companies HCA hired to take part in the airlift, these aircraft were military and could only be asked to take part. They flew one, maybe two, sorties on Thursday, and then, for reasons that aren't clear, broke off from the operation. The next morning CH-47s flew half a dozen round trips, effectively finishing the airlift.

The participation of the CH-47s was important because of their size. Most of the other helicopters helping Tulane could only carry between one and six people. There were a few civilian Blackhawks that took part in the airlift, and they could carry up to twenty people. The twin-rotor CH-47 Chinook, on the other hand, measures nearly a hundred feet from rotor to rotor and carries up to sixty people. "Chinooks were completely different than anything else we had ever seen before," said Kim Graham, who was helping to coordinate the evacuation from the garage. "You could hear them coming from far away and when they would land they would knock you over because they were so intense."

HCA and Tulane officials, and people working on behalf of HCA and Tulane, began trying to get large helicopters such as CH-47s as early as Tuesday. They eventually succeeded. But when the dust had settled, and the people who took part or experienced the Tulane airlift began retelling their stories, there were multiple accounts of just how this goal was achieved.

"There were all sorts of people who say they were the ones who made the earth move," said HCA executive Mel Lagarde, weeks after the Tulane airlift. "I can tell you that during this whole process there were a number of people offering to do this and do that. Whenever someone would tell me this I would say, 'Go right ahead and do what you can.' I never turned down any assistance."

It is, of course, quite possible that all of these accounts are true from the point of view of the person telling them. For instance, it is possible that someone might have taken steps to secure CH-47s, then seen one land on the parking garage deck an hour later, and then come to the understandable conclusion that their actions were what led to that aircraft's arrival, when in fact something else had done so. It is also quite possible that several things led to the presence of the CH-47s; that a person in authority decided to send aircraft after hearing about the need for them from multiple sources. Finally, it is always possible that a CH-47 took off from the Superdome or the airport intending to fly to Tulane and was diverted in the air to another destination, or a CH-47 got diverted while airborne to fly to Tulane. After all, rescue situations do not allow for careful documentation.

"There were helicopters showing up from all over," said HCA executive Sam Hazen. "A lot of them were the ones we hired, a lot of them were guys from the military who we somehow got, and for all we know, some of them were just independent pilots flying around to see what they could do. We may never know."

Recognizing that it might be impossible to ever know for certain how it was that these large military aircraft ended up on the deck of the Tulane Hospital, here are some of the stories about what may have led to the participation of the CH-47s:

From John Holland, who was directing helicopter traffic from the roof of the parking garage:

> When I was on my way into New Orleans and stopped to fuel, I got the phone number for something called Eagle Base or Eagle's Nest, which was the controlling agency for the military aircraft taking part in the overall New Orleans rescue [which was physically located at the Louisiana Superdome]. Well, by that afternoon I could see Chinooks flying all over New Orleans. And

so I called over to Eagle Base and talked to a Colonel Jensen over there and asked him for more aircraft.

I said to the Colonel, "My name is John Holland. I am a retired colonel and I am on top of Tulane Hospital. I see the aircraft going by, and if there is any way you could send an aircraft in here, it would help us out a lot. We need all the help we can get." A few minutes later they sent one or two of them over to do a quick lift.

From Dan Bitton, the EC-135 pilot from Chicago:

On Thursday afternoon, when I realized there was going to be a lot more lift needed, I made an unannounced landing at Eagle's Nest. I did call and ask for permission to land, and it was denied, but I stopped there anyway. I mean, what were they going to do? Shoot me down?

I walked right into this tent and there was a general there. I told him who I was and what I was doing, and what they needed over at Tulane. I asked for two CH-47s and a couple of Blackhawks, and he promised I'd get them. He said they'd land right about 1600 (four p.m.) A couple of hours later, they landed right about the time he'd said they would.

From Brad Smith, a Blackhawk pilot for the A-12 Medical Company of the Louisiana National Guard:

My daughter (a patient at Tulane) flew out on Wednesday and I flew out on Thursday. When I was still at Tulane, I called and talked to our flight operations center in Pineville, Louisiana, and passed on everything about Tulane, including the fact that the hospital needed military helicopters. They passed that information onto the emergency operations center in Baton Rouge.

I gave the phone number of our flight operations center to Jim Montgomery after that. After I got evacuated, I went to my military unit. For a while I was manning the phone. And guess who called Thursday night? Jim Montgomery. He was pretty upset because he had heard that the governor's office was saying Tulane had been evacuated, when of course it hadn't been. So I took down his message and called the emergency operations center in Baton Rouge again and told them again.

I have no idea whether these messages made a difference.[3]

From Karen Troyer-Caraway, who helped coordinate the Tulane staging area at Louis Armstrong Airport on Thursday:

I was with Bob Loup [the airport operations supervisor who drove around in the white pickup truck] all day. He was the one who taught me what a Chinook was and what a Blackhawk was.

At some point I saw one of the CH-47 pilots standing around and I went right up and talked to him. He was wearing one of those big helmets. And I knocked on it and he turned around and I introduced myself and I said "I really need one of these." And he said, "Oh, yeah Tulane Hospital! I've been seeing birds flying on and off the parking garage over there all day!" and I said, "Yeah, that's us. We really could use one of those." And he said to me, "I'll go make a run for you!" And he got back in his helicopter and took off.

I don't know for sure whether he ever got to Tulane, or

---

[3] Smith started flying helicopter missions in support of the relief efforts on Friday, and did so for about a week.

whether he came back with Tulane people. But I do know that a while later a CH-47 landed with people from Tulane.

Then there is the story that comes from the HCA corporate side. It was pieced together from the testimonies of Mel Lagarde and many people at HCA's offices in Tallahassee and Nashville. This saga does not account for the presence of CH-47s on Thursday. This being the case, one or more of the earlier reports may account for the presence of Chinooks on Thursday, while this story accounts for them on Friday.

According to this point of view, the saga of the CH-47s started on Tuesday, when HCA first began working to get clearance to use a privately owned, Russian-built, MI-8 helicopter to take part in the airlift. In an attempt to get FAA clearance for the MI-8, HCA executive Chuck Hall eventually made contact with someone in the Pentagon, who put him in touch with two Louisiana National Guard colonels. "We were really nagging them about the Russian helicopter, and in the process of doing that we eventually said to these colonels, 'Well, if we can't get this to fly, can we get help in another way?'" Hall said. "And through this process, these colonels got us the Chinooks. I think we were calling them so much that they were getting irritated with me.

"I know a lot of people were making phone calls. But I believe these colonels are the ones who really bailed us out."[4]

The two National Guard colonels told HCA they needed authorization from the governor's office to fly such missions. On Friday morning HCA government relations director David Critchlow spoke to Rochelle Dugas, a legislative director for Louisiana governor Kathleen Blanco. Governor Blanco ordered the CH-47s to assist in the Tulane evacuation, which they did that morning.

---

[4] Attempts to contact these colonels in the process of researching this book were unsuccessful.

Chapter Twelve
To the Garage

Now we've gotten ahead of ourselves. In describing the saga from the air, from corporate headquarters, from HCA's facilities in Lafayette, and from the Louis Armstrong Airport, it is important to remember that at the focus of this were a thousand hot, tired, dehydrated, confused, and at times demoralized people at Tulane Hospital. They watched small helicopters come and go all day Tuesday and Wednesday, carrying one or two patients at a time. They spent a third consecutive uncomfortable night in the hospital building Wednesday night. By Thursday morning most of the patients were gone – but that still left more than 80 percent of the people who had been there when the hurricane hit. None of them knew when they'd get out, or even if they'd get out.

So how did people survive and keep from panicking during the long days of waiting to be rescued? By keeping track of what was happening. By retaining their sense of humor. By not giving up hope. And by making friends. "We played games," said Melanie Ehrlich, a professor at the Tulane School of Medicine who waited in line all day Thursday with her husband to get on a helicopter. "We played hide the penny behind your back. We played toss the penny into the plastic cup. We sang songs. We talked and we made friends with people near us in line."

People also survived by drinking plenty of fluids and by eating occasionally, and in that regard they never had cause for concern. In New Orleans, after the Katrina flood, thousands of people were in desperate need of food and water. But the people at Tulane Hospital had plenty to eat and drink. "The doctors and nurses were very nice to us and gave us meals through the whole ordeal," said Peggy Taylor, a liver transplant patient who flew to Lafayette on Wednesday. "No one was starving."

Dawn Guidry, food services director at the hospital, said that on Sunday night her staff served hot food, plus they baked cakes and muffins that they served on Monday. "Then we were serving dry cereal and canned foods, like ravioli and Vienna sausages and fruit," she said. "When the helicopters started coming, they started bringing large quantities of Pop-Tarts and these ready-to-eat tuna packets. And of course we always had plenty of water to give out.

"The main thing to remember is we always served three meals a day, even after the power went out and after people started leaving by helicopter."

Serving meals was made all the more challenging by the fact that food services was constantly moving from one part of the hospital to another. In advance of the storm, it was moved from the ground floor to the fifth floor. After the hurricane came through, the staff moved it back to the ground floor. When the flooding began, it had to be moved back up to the fifth floor. "Sharif Omar knocked on my door and told me water was coming in," Guidry said. "So me, my chef, and six of our people moved the entire nonperishable kitchen back up to the fifth floor. It took us until six a.m., and after that we had to turn around and feed everyone." Later that day, with temperatures in the building going way up, the decision was made to move food service down to the second floor, where many people were being held in advance of the airlift. "Unfortunately there were no elevators by this time," Guidry said. "So we got nurses, doctors, everyone we could find, and we human-chained all the food down to the second floor.

"That was the kind of thing that happened over and over that week. There weren't any job titles. People did what they had to do."

People did their best in spite of the fact that there was a constant specter of danger. "Things generally seemed to be progressing all the while, but we were fully aware that at any time things could go very wrong very fast," said Lagarde. "I was worried about a helicopter crash; worried the building might catch on fire; worried patients might start to die from the heat; and worried someone might lose it and we'd have a riot on our hands."

A lot of the fears were security related. "We were very concerned that we had all the bases covered," said deputy chief of police Warren Breaux. "We were nervous that there might be someone sneaking onto the stairwell. And we were very worried that someone might sneak into another building around us with a rifle and take a shot at some of our people on the top of the garage for whatever reason."

There were also unspoken fears related to the hospital's deteriorating medical capability. "If a patient had a cardiac arrest right now, we certainly wouldn't be able to do anything for that patient," physician Jeff Myers said during an interview with National Public Radio on Wednesday.

On Wednesday and Thursday looking on the bright side wasn't easy. Tuesday night Tulane lost electrical power as provided by its supplemental "generator on wheels" that had been brought in by tractor-trailer. From that point on there was no light inside the building, except as provided by the sun, flashlight, or candle. There were also no operating phones, except for cellular phones and two land lines in the command center.

The loss of the tractor-trailer generator didn't mean the complete end of electrical power, however. Many pieces of medical equipment had backup batteries lasting up to a day. And, prior to the storm, the hospital had stored a couple of portable generators, and more were sent in by helicopter on Tuesday.[5]

One of the few places in Tulane Hospital that had nearby access to an exterior balcony was the neonatal intensive care unit. On Sunday night, before Katrina hit, hospital administrators had the foresight to move the rest of the electricity-dependent patients into that area and to station the gas-powered portable generators outside, with cables running inside. When central electrical power went down on Tuesday night, the generators were already in place to be turned on. "The idea to move those patients into that area in advance like that was an incredibly important decision," physician Bill Gill later said.

These portable generators operated on gasoline, and unfortunately the hospital did not have a big supply of such fuel. There were, however, hundreds of vehicles with gas in their tanks parked on the first few levels of the parking deck. So starting Tuesday night and continuing into Wednesday, people who worked for the hospital's plant operations department began siphoning gasoline out of every car they could find. The effort had no detractors. "Everyone knew what we were doing, and I didn't hear one person complain about this," said Sonny Breaux, a supervisor for the maintenance department. "Everyone gave us their keys and said to us, 'I've got plenty of gas. Take it out of my car.'

"We all knew what we had to do, which was keep patients alive."

---

[5] Steve Schaaf, whose daughter was one of the first to be evacuated by helicopter, did odd jobs on the roof of the garage Tuesday afternoon. Interviewed months later, Schaaf said that two of these portable generators were donated to Tulane by Air Logistics, helicopter company owned by Bristow Group Inc. that unexpectedly sent a helicopter to Tulane on Tuesday.

anic and fear were generally kept to a minimum at Tulane. But on Wednesday afternoon something occurred that scared many people. At around two o'clock in the afternoon a U.S. Army helicopter landed on the parking deck and dropped off a SWAT team consisting of about six or eight heavily armed soldiers. The SWAT team ran across the parking garage deck, down the stairs, and over to the hospital building, its members frantically yelling commands to everyone.

"We were all standing in the command center when suddenly this SWAT team comes tearing down from the garage," said Kiernan. "They all yelled, 'Freeze! Freeze!' and so we just had to stand there and not move while they went through the entire building, room by room."

Most people at the hospital weren't terribly inconvenienced by the SWAT team's forceful command to stay where they were (after all, most people had no place to go). But the moment the armed men arrived, a group of physicians and EMTs were transporting a very fragile patient who had just undergone a bone marrow transplant. "She wasn't going to be transported until her helicopter was within thirty minutes of landing," physician Steven Davidoff later recalled. "Finally I rounded up my team and we donned masks and gloves to protect her from us, since she had very few cells to fight infection with." After carrying her down the stairs, the team heard the inexplicable orders to stop moving. "We sat quietly next to our patient (still strapped to a back board resting on top of two chairs) and waited for the signal to resume our evacuation." The SWAT team's arrival also coincided with the presence of a group of boats from the Louisiana Department of Wildlife and Fisheries. In fact, the SWAT team's arrival slowed the pace of the ill-fated boat evacuation (which, ironically, turned out to be a good thing for the people at Tulane).

An hour and a half later, the SWAT team calmed down, explained that they had been sent there to react to rumors of a possible "hostage crisis," and proceeded to get back on their helicopter and leave. "I don't know about anyone else, but I was pretty mad because they didn't offer to help, or to even ask us if they needed us to take a message back to where they were going," Kiernan said.

"Then they left. And it was like, 'Who were those guys?' That was a weird moment."

Shortly after the SWAT team and the Wildlife and Fisheries left, the Tulane maintenance people climbed to the top of the hospital roof and draped a large American flag over the side of the building. As can happen in such crisis situations, the sight of the flag affected many people in a strong and very personal way. "A couple of doctors came to me in tears when they saw the flag hanging there," said Tulane vice president Jeff Tully.

The idea that a flag should be sent to Tulane was originally the idea of Chuck Hall, the head of HCA's North Florida division. "We were sending in all sort of supplies to New Orleans from helicopters that were taking off from Pensacola," Hall said. "One morning when I came in, it occurred to me that a big flag might help their morale, because I remembered the images of American flags after 9/11."

The 25-by-30-foot flag was folded and put in a box with a small note suggesting they hang it "like the one that was hung over the Pentagon after 9/11," or some such verbiage. But after the flag was taken out of the box, myths about its origins began. "The rumor began that this was the flag that flew over the Pentagon on 9/11," helicopter pilot John Holland later wrote. Physician Mike Kiernan said, "We were told it was sent to us from the White House and that it was a flag that flew over the Capitol at one time." The news media eventually got into the act. "A helicopter dropped off a large triangular shaped package addressed to the CEO of the [Tulane] hospital," the *Orange County* (California) *Register* later reported. "It was the flag from New York's Ground Zero."

Asked about the origins of the flag several months later, Hall said it had been procured by David Smith, director of contracting for the North Florida division. Smith, in turn, said he delegated the task to Elaine

Gimlin, supply director for West Florida Hospital in Pensacola.

As it turns out, Gimlin had obtained the flag from a seafood eatery in Pensacola called Joe Patti's Seafood. "They told us the situation and what they needed it for, and we were glad to help," said store manager Marie Patty Walker. "It was a real honor, really was."[6]

O n a grimmer note, people at Tulane soon became heavily involved in the ongoing saga of the Charity Hospital evacuation. As described previously, FEMA told Charity on Tuesday that it would soon be evacuated. But on Wednesday morning it became obvious to doctors at Charity Hospital that this wasn't going to happen in time for many of the hospital's more critical patients. Charity doctors Ben duBoisblanc and Francesco Simeone then brought four patients to Tulane, where they were evacuated by helicopter. On Thursday duBoisblanc and two other Charity physicians asked Tulane officials if they would assist in the evacuation of about twenty more patients. Mel Lagarde agreed, but asked duBoisblanc to bring the patients over in small groups. Because of logistics it didn't happen that way. Charity doctors and nurses arrived by boat and truck at the Tulane garage on Thursday afternoon with about forty patients.

Thus began the most controversial chapter in the Tulane airlift. The Charity patients arrived at the Saratoga garage about the time Tulane's last patients were being evacuated. Because of this, the small helicopters configured for medical uses had begun to go to other hospitals, and they were

---

[6] The story about the flag wasn't the only large inaccuracy that made its way into the media. The *Chicago Tribune* reported that armed "thugs" made their way into hospital at one point, which never happened. The *Houston Chronicle* reported that Tulane patients were still being evacuated on Saturday, when the last Tulane patient actually left on Thursday. National networks reported on Wednesday morning that Charity had been evacuated. The list goes on and on.

being replaced in the Tulane airlift by large, military helicopters configured to carry upright, healthy people. "What really drove things at this point is what kind of helicopter we had and where it was going," said Kiernan. "If the helicopter only had seats bolted to the floor, then it couldn't take a stretcher patient." Compounding this problem was the fact that many of these large, military helicopters were only authorized to fly to the airport, where conditions were much worse than they were at Tulane. Having seen conditions there, Tulane did not think it wise to just take patients to the airport and drop them off there.

Add the fatigue and confusion everyone was experiencing, and misunderstandings were inevitable. In fact, some of Charity's patients and doctors were not evacuated until about 9 p.m. On at least one occasion duBoisblanc went up to the top level of the garage and exchanged harsh words with Lagarde. "He [duBoisBlanc] was mad at me and I was mad as hell back at him," Lagarde later said. "We definitely traded words, to say the least."

Asked about the exchange months later, duBoisBlanc had this to say: "It was hard for me to watch helicopters taking off and landing full of ambulatory patients while we had critically ill patients there. I have since heard the explanation for this, and I understand it, and it makes some sense. But as far as why I got testy, you have to understand that these patients were my moral and ethical responsibility, and I took the Hippocratic Oath to defend the interest of these people. So I thought that the right thing to do was see to it that the squeaky wheel got the grease."

That day duBoisblanc aired his point of view to CNN reporter Sanjay Gupta, who had arrived at the Tulane parking garage early that afternoon. The resulting story did not paint HCA and Tulane in a positive light and was still a sore spot for people associated with Tulane months after the ordeal. "We watched as non-essential personnel from Tulane… were evacuated while patients from Charity Hospital were still standing by," Gupta said on CNN the next day. "Patients who were requiring mechanical ventilation with a bag actually forcing air into their lungs – they were standing by – while some of the other personnel were being evacuated, and that was certainly surprising to us. I'm not sure exactly what the reason is, maybe there is one."

Misunderstandings aside, the sight of the Saratoga garage was grim that day. On Tuesday and Wednesday patients generally stayed in the organized and relatively private confines of Tulane Hospital until it was time for them to leave, when they were carried, pushed, or escorted to the top of the garage with some degree of dignity and order. But on Thursday the Charity patients – most of them in critical condition – were strewn about all over the seventh floor of the parking garage awaiting their departure. "Many of the patients had been on ventilators; they were being hand-bagged by respiratory therapists, nurses, and other personnel, who took turns in the stifling heat," physician Nancy Ross-Ascuitto wrote. "Physicians and nurses were intensely busy. Our son saw a diabetic patient with legs amputated in severe distress. He asked, 'Dad, does that lady have legs? Is she going to die?'"

The situation was made all the more emotional by the fact that two of the patients Charity had brought over died while waiting to be evacuated. According to Charity student nurse Susan Sanborn, one of those two patients actually wasn't registered at her hospital when Katrina hit; she had arrived by boat from an abandoned nursing home the day of the flood. "I am positive about this because I was there when they unloaded her," Sanborn said.

It is also important to remember that there were about a thousand people at the Tulane garage by around Thursday at noon, all of whom wanted badly to leave. "I had no shortage of people bitching about not being able to get on helicopters by this time," Lagarde said. Sharif Omar, who was running back and forth telling people how many passengers, and what type of passengers, each helicopter could carry, had this to say about the subject: "Toward the end of it I did have some people come to me crying because they thought I was the one who was choosing who was going on each plane," he said. "But really we were just going by the order in which they were already lined up."

Also lost in the frenzy of that long day was the fact that many Tulane doctors, nurses, and staff were trying to help Charity patients, and that Tulane gave Charity's patients every bit of bottled oxygen, drugs, food, and water that the hospital still had. "We [Charity's staff] would send six patients or so over to Tulane in the big truck, and then when it went back to Charity, they [Tulane's staff] would load it down with bottled water and granola bars," said Jennifer McGee, a resident surgeon at Charity.

Melanie Ehrlich, a medical school professor who waited in line for a spot on a helicopter Thursday, later said she was very impressed by how much Tulane people did to help the Charity patients. "As we stood near the back of the line Thursday morning, we were told that patients from Charity were being driven up the driveway to the helicopter platform on the roof, so we would have to make a path for them," she later said. "A Tulane Security guard alerted us by shouting 'Make a hole! Patients coming!' Those of us on the bottom end of the line chanted 'Make a hole!' and the chant was continued enthusiastically up the line of weary people, and this happened over and over again. There was no sense of resentment of patient evacuation, whether they were from Charity or Tulane.

"We witnessed Tulane doctors, nurses, orderlies, and even family members of doctors working extraordinarily hard under third-world conditions to save those patients."

Chapter Thirteen
The Last Twenty-four Hours

T hursday afternoon, when a CH-47 Chinook landed on the Saratoga parking deck and took off with about sixty people on board, it appeared as if the Tulane airlift was winding down. With Chinooks now involved in the rescue, and with the staging area at the Louis Armstrong Airport a mere fifteen-minute flight away, it seemed only a matter of hours before everyone would be gone.

The evacuation now took on more of a frantic pace. Unlike the small medical evacuation helicopters that had dominated the airlift on Tuesday and Wednesday, the pilots of the large military aircraft were not prepared to wait long once they landed. "We had to get people lined up and ready to go because those guys don't wait around for anything," Sharif Omar said.

With people moving out faster, and with the situation in downtown New Orleans deteriorating, Tulane officials decided to move everyone from the hospital building to the parking garage. "Our security people, who did an absolutely marvelous job, were really pushing me to get everyone out of the hospital and onto the parking deck," said Mel Lagarde. "I mean, there are only four stairwells and one entrance ramp to the parking deck. But there were many entrances to the hospital building. We were worried about people trying to break in to get drugs or simply trying to break in to loot."

Security did a floor-by-floor search. By the time it got dark, Tulane Hospital's buildings were locked down. Doors with electrically powered magnetic locks were secured by use of chains and padlocks.

At that point everyone was hoping they'd be out of New Orleans within a few hours. To the dismay of Tulane and HCA officials, however, the airlift didn't pick up speed on Thursday evening, but tapered off. While no one knows for sure why the CH-47s first came to Tulane on Thursday afternoon, no one knows for sure why they flew only one or two sorties that day. As for the larger civilian helicopters, one pilot said he stopped flying because of fatigue. "We stopped flying on Thursday night because we needed sleep," said Chuck Brainerd, pilot of a civilian Blackhawk that flew about half a dozen sorties on Thursday. "We had been flying all day and it was late and it was dark."

It would be hard to overstate just how demoralizing this news was to people still stuck at Tulane – most of whom had been herded into long lines by this time. "Standing for hours and hours and hours, the line moved inch-by-inch to nowhere," pediatric cardiologist Bob Ascuitto later wrote. "Toward the afternoon, some helicopters began to arrive, and our spirits started to lift. After several hours, our family was placed in the group designated to be airlifted next. We were herded into a stairwell leading up to the roof.

"The heat and stench in that stairwell were overwhelming, and some of us began to feel ill. A nurse with us who was pregnant had to be treated.

"Then we heard the most depressing news. A hospital administrator announced that no more helicopters were coming…We would need to spend the night in the hospital garage."

To compound the frustration of not getting out, Tulane officials heard yet another erroneous news report. "I called my wife, and she told me Governor Blanco had announced that Tulane had been totally evacuated," Jim Montgomery said. "According to my count she was about four hundred people short in her analysis." Fearful that the story might result in a loss of helicopters, Montgomery quickly got on the phone to tell everyone from the Louisiana National Guard to the Louisiana Hospital Association that Tulane people were still in downtown New Orleans. Among the people he spoke with that night was Brad Smith, a National Guard pilot who had been at Tulane only a day earlier.

There was, of course, no going back to the Tulane Hospital building. At around one a.m. the remaining Tulane staffers and family members settled down to what they hoped would be a quiet night under the stars. "Everyone crowded together on the garage's concrete floor," physician Bob Ascuitto wrote. "No pillows, no blankets. There were no restroom facilities. People had to use stairwells and parts of the garage as latrines. The odors emanating from these areas were horrific.

"Despite the deplorable conditions, no one really cared anymore. Just get us the hell out of here."

But the night was full of interruptions. The first unexpected visitor was from FEMA (the first representative of the federal government since Sunday night's visit from the Department of Homeland Security official who was scouting locations for a DMAT unit). The man arrived by helicopter and announced he would be directing an air evacuation from there the next day. "His first name was Doug, and he really looked official," Lagarde said. "He had a name tag with a photo ID and a satellite phone and everything. And he told us that the next day, eight helicopters would be assisting both us and Charity in the evacuation and that he would be in charge of that operation."

About an hour later a U. S. Marine sergeant named Kraft arrived by helicopter and said he was there to help defend Charity Hospital. With the help of plant operations head George Jamison, Kraft worked his way back into Tulane Hospital, then across the street to Charity. A few hours later he came back to the Tulane garage. He then proceeded to pace back and forth along on the retaining walls of the garage, keeping a lookout for looters from that point onward.[7]

Then came what was, for many people, the most frightening moment of the entire ordeal. At about 4:30 in the morning everyone heard a rumbling sound coming from the east. "Then we looked over and could see that the sky in one direction was changing color to orange," Tulane's Jeff Tully said. "I thought we were under siege. It really looked as if someone was bombing the city." Charity physician Jennifer McGee, who spent that night on the roof of the garage, said the explosion made her seriously question whether she was going to get out. "I thought I was going to die," she said. "In fact, I knew I was going to die when that thing blew up. I mean, keep in mind that we had no idea what it was. Some people thought it was a terrorist act. Some figured it was a helicopter or plane crash. All we could see was water everywhere, and the explosion. I mean, people were really at their wit's end."

What everyone found out later is that they had witnessed a warehouse explosion on the industrial edge of New Orleans.

Tulane's representative at Louis Armstrong Airport had an even more frightening night. On Thursday the facility became even more overrun with evacuees than it had been the day before. "I'm not really sure where everyone was coming from, and I didn't notice this while it was happening, because I was so focused on what we were

---

[7] Unfortunately no one ever learned Sergeant Kraft's first name.

doing," Kim Ryan said. "But by the end of the day the airport was full of all sorts of people.

"There were thousands of patients on the floor in various states of duress, and not nearly enough people to take care of them. Then, in another part of the terminal, there were thousands of evacuees. Now there was some water at the airport because the airport uses well water, but there obviously weren't enough bathrooms for everyone, and people were just using the bathroom wherever. So by this time there were feces and urine just on the floor. And there was some security, but not nearly enough."

By about ten p.m. on Thursday there were five Tulane-chartered buses left – three full of Tulane people and two that were empty and awaiting more helicopter riders they hoped would eventually arrive. The bus drivers, whose day had begun sixteen hours earlier in Houston, were ready to leave. "They were in my face telling me that they didn't sign up for this, that the situation was getting unsafe and that they had to get their buses out of there," Ryan said.

By this time word that Tulane had two empty buses had made its way through the airport. And this turned out to be a very good thing for the staff and family members of another New Orleans-area hospital.

Chalmette Medical Center was a 230-bed facility about nine miles east of downtown New Orleans, in St. Bernard Parish. The storm surge buried the facility, owned by Pennsylvania-based Universal Health Services, under an estimated thirteen feet of water. Without power and telephones, and unable to get in touch with their parent company, Chalmette's staff on Tuesday and Wednesday evacuated its fifty-two patients to the St. Bernard jail with the help of the local fire department. "I honestly don't know where the patients went from there, but when I got to the airport I later found out that several of them were there," Chalmette's chief operating officer Tim Coffey said months later. While awaiting help, four Chalmette patients died at the hospital. "I would say that the temperature in our facility got to 110 or 120 degrees," Coffey said.

Late Thursday morning National Guard helicopters evacuated Chalmette's remaining staff, family members of staff, and family members of patients – 138 people in all – to the Louis Armstrong Airport. When they got there, they assumed they had been rescued. But after waiting in the baggage claim area for five hours without any explanation, they realized their problems weren't over. "Finally, it hit me about 5:30 that evening that no one knew we were there; that the airport had no mechanism to manage the people who were coming into the facility; and that we were basically stranded," Coffey said.

Coffey tracked down a Homeland Security official who told him there were buses being loaded at another end of the airport. "But he didn't know whose buses they were, or who they were taking away, or where they were going," he said. Coffey worked his way across the building and tracked down Tulane's Kim Ryan. "I told her my story and she told me her story," he said. "And when she told me that it was beginning to look as if their people weren't going to make it that night, I asked her if we could put our own people on those buses."

Ryan's account of the conversation was more dramatic. "He comes running toward me begging us to sell or loan him our two remaining buses," Ryan said. "He is in tears and he says that he has all these employees and family members and they are not safe there at the airport."

Ryan called Sam Hazen at HCA's corporate office in Nashville. It was, according to everyone at HCA's headquarters in Nashville, the first time they had even heard the name "Chalmette" since New Orleans flooded. Nevertheless the decision to assist Chalmette's employees was an easy one. With bus drivers threatening to leave at any moment, Ryan told Coffey, and Coffey told his co-workers, to move quickly, which is why they literally ran through the airport. "It was very unnerving because, by this time, there were easily twenty thousand people in the airport; maybe more," he said. "There were people everywhere, and some of them were trying to come with us but we couldn't let them come with us. And, meanwhile, there were two people in our group who were missing family members. So there was an enormous panic while we were trying to track those people down."

The sight of all the people in the airport horrified Coffey. "It was one of the most horrific things I have ever seen with regard to the loss of humanity and the loss of dignity," he said. "There were literally people who were on stretchers dying and no one even noticed. It was a very sad thing."

The Chalmette staff made it. Within a few minutes, all 138 of them were on board air-conditioned buses and on their way to Lafayette.

Kim Ryan, Cheryl Turano, and Karen Troyer-Caraway all assumed it was time for them to board buses and go to Lafayette as well. But then, at the last minute, Hazen called Ryan and told her she needed to get the staging area ready for the next morning. Ryan did what she was told and got off the bus as it was pulling out. She told her daughter Cheryl to go to Lafayette without her and tried to find Troyer-Caraway, who was on another bus. But she couldn't find her, which is why Kim Ryan spent Thursday night alone at the airport. "And it was by far the most traumatic night for me," she said. "By this time the airport was just packed with people, some of whom were hospital patients who were moaning and not being cared for, others of whom were evacuees who were getting restless.

"People were using the bathroom wherever they wanted to. Meanwhile it was freezing cold because they had set up these air conditioners to keep the place cool and they were overdoing it. Some medical people were trying to cover patients with cardboard to keep people from dying of hypothermia because it was so cold."

Ryan found a medical command tent set up inside the terminal. "There was a military guard in fatigues and with a semi-automatic, and I asked him if I could sleep there." Ryan couldn't find a blanket, but she located some cellophane wrap that had been used to wrap supplies. "I wrapped myself in it and laid down on the ground."

Back in Nashville, meanwhile, Hazen was very worried. "I really didn't mean for Kim to get off that bus, and certainly not to stay at the airport by herself," he later said. "So after we got off the phone I sat here until two or three in the morning trying to connect with the folks in Lafayette and with anyone else that I could find to see if I could find Kim.

"Finally Kim called us very late and said she was safe. I was quite relieved. And I can tell you that the entire day – which started with us getting the buses from Houston and ended with Kim's call – was the longest day of my life."

F riday would be the smoothest day of the week as far as the evacuation was concerned. The first helicopters began showing up at Tulane at about eight a.m., and within a few hours the four hundred remaining people had been evacuated. It was now time to take care of the pets, and there were seventy-nine of them – including dogs, cats, birds, and a lizard. Some, but not all of them, were in cages. "My last run consisted of nine passengers, five dogs, and three cats," pilot Greg Miller said. "Each of the animals was being held by a passenger or was on a leash. Most of them just sat there and were good. None of them took a dump on my helo, so that was good."

In spite of all the setbacks, a wave of conviviality and energy overcame the people still left at Tulane. Several of them took pictures that morning in which everyone seemed to be smiling. Almost everyone left at this point was either a Tulane staffer or a family member of a Tulane staffer – family members of patients mostly left on Thursday. Many people found it hard to get used to the idea of having no one to take care of. "I will never forget it," Joe Lasky said. "People *cleaned* the parking garage. They picked up every scrap of litter or paper or mess and covered up the things someone else would have to clean up later. It was as if the people who were left were eager to do something good at this point, and there wasn't anything to do but clean the parking garage."

No one is exactly certain how many round trips the CH-47s and Blackhawks made that day. But it all went smoothly, and everyone remembers how wonderful it was to get to the airport, be handed a bottle of water and a granola bar, and be directed onto an air-conditioned bus. "It was a marvelously choreographed dance," physician Marta Rozans later said. "And I'll never forget what my son said when they gave him a cold drink. He said, 'Can I have another one?'"

In the process HCA officials did not forget the hospital across the street. After Thursday's events and media coverage, HCA officials from Jack Bovender on down wanted to make certain they had done everything in their power to assist in the evacuation of Charity. They passed on this sentiment to Lagarde and Montgomery, who agreed. Early Friday morning Montgomery met with several Charity doctors who were in the Tulane garage, including duBoisblanc, and told them Charity's people were welcome to use the garage to airlift out the remaining patients and staff. They also told Charity representatives they were welcome to use every bit of food, water, and medical supplies Tulane's staff was leaving behind. "Many of their physicians shook my hand and told me how grateful they were to us for what we had done," Montgomery said.

After all he'd been through, Mel Lagarde was understandably anxious to leave with the rest of his Tulane staffers. But at the last minute HCA's corporate office asked him to remain behind for a few hours – again, just to make absolutely certain Tulane had done everything within its power to help Charity. A few people stayed with him – including helicopter pilot Stiles Clarke, amateur radio operator Theo Titus, Marine Sergeant Kraft, and physician Lee Hamm. "Mel didn't ask me to stay, but I saw that he was staying behind, and I thought he might need someone with medical training," Hamm said. At 11:20 a.m. they watched a

Blackhawk lift off, carrying Jim Montgomery, Danita Sullivan, Jeff Tully, Sharif Omar, Kim Graham, and even the FEMA representative (whose eight helicopters never showed up).

From a suddenly very empty garage, Lagarde got in touch with a Charity physician through a phone patch arranged by HCA's corporate headquarters. He explained that the last of Tulane's staff and doctors had left, but that Charity was welcome to use everything Tulane was leaving behind, including the services of Clarke, who could possibly raise helicopters on the radio.

In the meantime a boat arrived at Tulane from the Department of Wildlife and Fisheries, carrying three patients from University Hospital but no doctors or nurses. "It suddenly occurred to me that there had been a communication breakdown and that these other hospitals didn't realize we didn't have people to take care of patients anymore," Lagarde said. Clarke got on the radio to make arrangements to have the patients airlifted out. And, since the men only had one truck to haul three patients, Sergeant Kraft decided to be resourceful. "That's the only time I've ever seen a U.S. Marine try to hot-wire a truck," Hamm said.

No sooner did they evacuate those three patients than two more showed up from Charity, this time with a nurse. They then arranged to have those two airlifted.

By this time it was around one in the afternoon, and Lagarde wanted to take a boat over to Charity, where he hoped to once and for all find someone in charge. But about this time members of the Department of Wildlife and Fisheries got a "stand-down" order. "I think that there had been some sniper fire or something, so they were told to stay in place for about half an hour or so," Hamm said. When the stand-down order was lifted, the boat driver told Lagarde he could take them to Charity, but he wouldn't be able to wait for them. "I didn't get on that boat and go over there because, to be honest, I wasn't sure how I'd get back," Lagarde said. Finally Clarke called in a Blackhawk, which took the men to Lakeview

Regional Medical Center in Covington. As they lifted off, they saw the lone figure of Sergeant Kraft, standing alone with his M-16 on the roof of the garage.

W ith Tulane's patients, family members, and employees away from the flooded hospital, HCA's focus shifted to getting them to Lafayette and helping them get on with their lives. But there was still plenty of activity at the Saratoga garage.

A few minutes after Lagarde's helicopter took off, duBoisblanc arrived back at the top of the garage, bringing with him about half a dozen patients and a few nurses. They found Dan Bitton and his EC-135. Bitton ferried another load of Charity people across Lake Pontchartrain to Lakeview in Covington, and radioed a couple of military pilots who came in and did the same. After getting those patients evacuated, duBoisblanc went back over to Charity. By that time a convoy of National Guard trucks had arrived to evacuate the hospital. "The cavalry was finally there," duBoisblanc said.

On Saturday there were evacuees, including some hospital patients, on the roof of the garage. (It is unclear how they got there or with what institution they were affiliated.) Among them were a woman and her three-year-old daughter, who had a tracheotomy valve in her throat, and some elderly patients who might have come from a nursing home.

There were also members of the Tennessee Air National Guard at the garage. They were directing Blackhawk helicopters sent from the 4th Infantry Division in Fort Hood, Texas, to evacuate people from New Orleans. One of the helicopters that landed contained *Houston Chronicle* reporter Michael Hedges. "There was mass confusion on the roof," said Hedges, who had previously been imbedded with the division when it was in Iraq. "We landed and we even went into the hospital, which clearly looked like a place that had just been hastily evacuated. You could see that there were people's belongings everywhere, this sort of thing."

Hedges, the Blackhawk crew members, and the Tennessee Air National Guardsmen were under the impression that the people they were evacuating were associated with Tulane. The *Chronicle* reported as much the next day. "At the time that seemed obvious," Hedges said. "But during the next few days while I was in New Orleans, it became more and more obvious that no one knew what was going on there or anywhere else. You cannot even imagine the situation down there."

Chapter Fourteen
Petty Cash and Plane Tickets

The most harrowing part of the rescue was over. Patients had been transferred to other hospitals. Now HCA had to deal with busload after busload of evacuees – more than a thousand of them. They were on their way to Lafayette, a medium-size city in central Louisiana with two HCA hospitals (Southwest Medical Center and Women's and Children's Hospital).

To decontaminate, feed, shelter, clothe, and assist these evacuees was a Herculean effort overseen by Kathy Bobbs, CEO at Women's and Children's Hospital. Asked about the enterprise later, Bobbs said she couldn't remember the precise moment she realized that she and the other HCA employees in Lafayette were going to have to do this. "But I do remember thinking we had twelve hours to create two shelters full of beds and food and everything else we needed," she said. "So I called my staff together and we got to it."

By the time the first busloads of people showed up Thursday afternoon, a large "decontamination station" had been set up at Southwest. When people arrived, they were sent into one of thirty-nine hospital rooms to bathe (after each person was finished, the bathrooms were disinfected). Then they were taken to one of two air-conditioned shelters which between the two of them had seven hundred large air mattresses, plus sheets, pillows, and pillowcases. Each shelter had catered food and pre-paid cellular phones in abundance. Each had shuttle buses coming and going that could take evacuees where they needed to go. Each had people standing by to help.

It was, according to Chalmette COO Tim Coffey, "very impressive. I mean, to walk into a room after being in the chaos of New Orleans and see hundreds of air mattresses set up – it was really something."

Deborah Spell, chief nursing officer at Southwest, said that to stock the shelters, her staff raided every store in Lafayette. "We went to Wal-Mart, K-Mart, Old Navy, and the grocery stores and we bought water and snack foods and underwear and diapers and children's clothes," she said. "We told everyone to keep the receipts and we would settle up with them later. And before we knew it, we had supplies all over the place." Since most of HCA's employees in Lafayette were dealing with the influx of patients, many of the people who ran the shelters were volunteers. "Family members of employees volunteered in droves – husbands, wives, teenage kids," said Bobbs.

Some volunteers went way beyond the call of duty. Perhaps the best example was Fred DeJean, the husband of Jayne DeJean, director of nursing resources for Women's and Children's Hospital. Fred DeJean, who sells pharmaceutical supplies for Amgen, spent all of Wednesday and Thursday loading supplies into helicopters. "The helos would come and unload babies and patients, then we'd pack them full of food and water and other things, and they'd take off," he later said. At about two a.m. on Friday morning, he was about to go home when Bobbs told him they desperately needed volunteers to work security for the buses going back to the Louis Armstrong Airport in three hours. DeJean started calling his friends, and within a couple of hours he had organized Lafayette's version of the "irregular" police force. "Being South Louisiana, it wasn't hard to find men who owned guns," he later said. DeJean and the rest of his group then rode to New Orleans, providing armed protection for the buses on Friday. "Without Fred and his friends, we wouldn't have had security on those buses," Bobbs said.

A few days later DeJean volunteered to provide security for an HCA-commissioned helicopter that went back to Tulane in an attempt to retrieve stem cells needed for cancer treatment.

Predictably, not everything related to the shelters went as expected. Bobbs and other HCA officials knew people coming from New Orleans would need clothes, shelter, and help getting on their way. But they didn't expect so few of them to have identification or money. "We were surprised at how few of them had IDs," said Yonnie Chesley, one of about a dozen human resources officials who flew down to Lafayette from HCA's corporate office in Nashville to help operate the shelters. Since it made more sense to hand out money than to keep people in shelters for weeks, petty cash became something else HCA distributed. The company gave away somewhere in the range of twenty-five thousand dollars to people based on stated need, and the honor code, during the next couple of days.

Chesley later said that when she was on her way to Lafayette, she imagined she'd be answering questions about human resources issues such as benefits and payroll. But that's not what happened. "I was making up beds, fitting pillowcases on pillows, and trying make sure we didn't run out of food and toilet paper."

Chesley was also surprised by the emotional state of the evacuees. "We thought people might be having emotional breakdowns because they had lost everything they owned," she said. "But we didn't really see that as much as we thought we would.

"When they got off the bus and got into that shelter, they were so happy to have been rescued. We heard that especially from some of the Charity people. They were so appreciative of HCA for saving their lives. They were so grateful to have a hot meal and a bed, because they had nothing. I can't tell you how appreciative they all were."

The biggest logistical hassle was getting people on their way. Many evacuees were picked up by family members on Friday and Saturday. But most of them had to be bussed, or flown, to destinations across the country – yet another expense HCA incurred as a part of the Hurricane Katrina rescue. On Saturday the company chartered three 727 airplanes to take people to Houston, Atlanta, or Newark, New Jersey, based on their final destination. From there everyone who needed it was given air fare (the company purchased 210 plane tickets). "This was by far the most difficult part of the whole process," said Chesley. "We basically got 980 people who had no money and no means of support where they needed to go in less than two days.

"By Saturday evening most everyone was gone and the shelters were empty."

Melanie Ehrlich, a professor at Tulane School of Medicine, was one of many people taken care of at the shelters. "We got rid of our nasty clothes and they gave us scrubs and booties and a shower," she said. "Then we got to the shelter and we got some sleep. Then we got some clothes out of the free pile. Then they gave my husband and I $100 each and paid to have us flown to New York.

"To be honest, HCA treated us so well that it was a shock when we got to the airport and were treated rudely by the guards who work for Homeland Security."

Of course, not everyone needed to go to a distant destination. Many preferred to stay in Louisiana, within driving distance of what was left of their homes, possessions, and offices in the New Orleans area. During the next few weeks and months many of these people stayed with friends and family members, a large percentage of whom were associated with HCA. "A huge number of employees brought people into their homes," said Leona Boullion. "This happened so fast that many of these people didn't even spend a night at a shelter."

There is an aspect to all this free shelter, free food, free cash, and free plane tickets that bears noting at this point. The people who set up and operated the shelters in Lafayette were focused on what they had to do. They didn't ask anyone who they were and whether they were associated with Tulane Hospital. Meanwhile many of the people who were evacuated by HCA-chartered buses from the Louis Armstrong Airport to HCA's hospitals in Lafayette originally had nothing to do with Tulane or with HCA. These people found themselves the recipients of unexpected corporate generosity.

The largest such group, by far, comprised people associated with Chalmette Hospital. One hundred and thirty-eight Chalmette employees were stranded at Louis Armstrong Airport late Thursday night. At the last minute HCA executive Sam Hazen and Tulane COO Kim Ryan let Chalmette's staff board two buses that HCA had originally intended for Tulane evacuees. "It was a long ride," Chalmette COO Tim Coffey later said. "We took the back route, but somehow we got out." During the drive someone from HCA stood up at the front of the bus and explained what would happen when the bus arrived in Lafayette. "They said we'd be decontaminated; we'd get a tetanus shot; we'd get [the prescription antibiotic] Cipro; we'd get new clothes and toiletries; we'd get a good night's rest; and that they they'd help us get where we needed to go."

When the Chalmette people arrived at Lafayette, they were given showers, just like the Tulane employees. They were given a hot meal and a place to sleep, just like the Tulane employees. They were given spending money and a bus or plane ticket to the destination of their choice, just like the Tulane employees. "They never asked us any questions about where we were from," Coffey said. "But they knew we were doctors and nurses and employees of Chalmette Medical Center. They were well aware of that. But we weren't treated any differently."

Two months after the hurricane Universal Health decided not to reopen Chalmette and to dismiss its staff. Interviewed several months after that news, Coffey said that he and the rest of the Chalmette people were very much in HCA's debt. "I cannot thank HCA enough," he said.

The degree to which HCA assisted other organizations' employees went largely unnoticed in the weeks after the evacuation. But in terms of corporate benevolence to a single individual, there was perhaps no better poster child than Susan Sanborn. When Katrina hit, Sanborn was a student nurse at Charity Hospital, one of the many people who did shifts "hand-bagging" patients to keep them alive after the electricity failed. On Friday afternoon Sanborn escorted a Charity patient who was airlifted from the Saratoga garage to HCA's Lakeview Regional Medical Center in Covington.

When she got to Covington, Sanborn was herded into a line, given a tetanus shot, an antibiotics shot, food, and water. She began socializing with some doctors she knew who worked at both Tulane and Charity. Before she knew it, she was on an HCA bus to Lafayette. "It was only after we got to Lafayette that this other nurse and I realized that we were two of the small number of Charity people there," she said. "And some of the Tulane doctors knew us, but they didn't say anything. So to be honest, we just kind of hid our little Charity Hospital badges." Sanborn spent that night in an HCA shelter. The next day the company gave her a plane ticket to Columbus, Ohio, where her parents lived.

A few weeks later Sanborn was watching a CNN special about Hurricane Katrina and became furious when the documentary implied that HCA had behaved unethically regarding its treatment of Charity Hospital. "Watching it really disgusted me, because that's just not what happened," she said. She tried to call CNN, to no avail. Then she dug through a packet of information HCA had given her during her evacuation process, went to the company's web site, and typed out an email to the company thanking it for all it had done for her.

That email eventually made its way to HCA human resources executive Donna Yurdin, then to CEO Jack Bovender. And after Yurdin looked into Sanborn's situation, the company decided to help the student nurse finish her training. (HCA did, after all, have a scholarship program because of the nursing shortage.) "When I heard this, I just started crying," Sanborn said. "They really didn't have to do this, but they did." Meanwhile, Sanborn said, the last thing she received related to Charity Hospital was her paycheck for time she worked in the hospital during and after Hurricane Katrina.

Resident surgeon Jennifer McGee was another Charity person evacuated by helicopter to the airport, then from the airport to the HCA shelter in Lafayette. "We were well aware of who was paying to get us out of there and who was paying to clean us up afterwards," McGee said. "And we heard about the things that were being said on CNN, and we knew that they were a disservice."

Finally, some of the policy decisions made by HCA's corporate office throughout this ordeal should be noted. About a year earlier, after so many hurricanes hit Florida, HCA had created the HCA Hope Fund to help its employees in need pay for expenses related to disaster, extended illness or injury, or other situations. HCA donated four million dollars in corporate money to it, and the fund then grew by another two million dollars through donations by employees, vendors, and physicians. "It isn't just for hurricane victims, although the fund came out of the hurricane experiences," said Jennifer Neely, community relations coordinator for HCA. Within the first six months the fund, run by an employee board of directors, made more than four thousand grants totaling $1.9 million.

HCA also announced that its employees displaced by Katrina would remain on its payroll until they were offered a legitimate job or the end of 2005, whichever came first. After that time, each employee would receive six weeks of severance pay.

These two corporate moves ensured that HCA's Gulf Coast employees had an opportunity to recover from the brutal effects of Hurricane Katrina. "This is an important part of the culture of this company," said CEO Jack Bovender. Bovender was astounded at the impact that Katrina and the company's reaction to it had on his company. In the days of the disaster and the days immediately following it, he sent out a few emails to everyone in the company, detailing what was happening and some of the things being done by HCA's employees to help. "At the time I had no idea what impact those emails would have on our company," he later said. "But it was absolutely amazing. On the emails I told people not to respond to me, but they did anyway. And people still come up to me and tell me that they read those emails."

Perhaps the most important HCA policy move, in terms of helping the city of New Orleans, was the decision to re-open Tulane Hospital as soon as possible. About two weeks after the evacuation, with flood waters in New Orleans just about subsided, Tulane staff began returning to the facility. Hospital vice president Rob Heifner was among the first to go back and remembered it this way:

> A couple of inches of water were still on the first floor, and it was very slippery and hazardous to walk on the tiled floors. The carpeted areas were completely ruined and there was mold growing out of the carpets, growing up the walls, and was even engulfing the ceilings as well. The humidity and heat inside the building was oppressive. The contents of offices and file rooms were unrecognizable in some areas. Desks and chairs were turned over,

papers drenched, equipment rusted and moldy.

The air was very musty, sort of like walking into a locker room, and added to that were odors that were combinations of weeks-old garbage, chemicals, human waste, and medical waste. I was there on that first trip with the insurance adjustor and the project director for the remediation company. One of them had to leave the building after about five minutes because of the smell, which I thought was odd since his business was disaster cleanup. We all had to wear respirators to be able to stay inside for any length of time.

We cracked into our three walk-in freezers in our kitchen about three weeks later, and the odor from those could be smelled throughout the entire building. It was the most awful thing I have ever smelled. Anyone who was there at the time won't soon forget it.

Rebuilding began in October. HCA hired a company to scrub every inch of the structure; wash or throw away every mattress, pillowcase, and piece of furniture in the building; and sanitize every surgical instrument in every doctor's office. The bottom floor had to be completely gutted – the walls removed and rebuilt. By mid-October, six weeks after the flood, more than nine hundred people (all wearing masks and decontamination suits) were cleaning and renovating the hospital building. The Tulane staff, meanwhile, had begun the laborious chore of moving their functions to another location, while overseeing the reconstruction of their facilities at Tulane.

This project was virtually unique in downtown New Orleans in October and November 2005, and in sharp contrast to the lack of activity in other parts of the city.

From this point on there are individual stories of patients who got better or got worse; people who began assessing the damage to their homes and cars; and people who felt lucky to be reunited with their loved ones. "I didn't know it at the time, but I pretty much lost everything in the flood," said Kim Graham, director of pediatric services at Tulane. "My house was in Lakeview, near a levee, and it was flooded in ten feet of water.

"But at least I finally got in touch with my husband, who had taken our two kids to Jackson [Mississippi]. During the entire experience of being at Tulane, I had never been able to get hold of him, and you can imagine how worried I was."

Times were also difficult for those whose close family members lost their possessions. "Just about everyone in my family, except me, lost everything," said respiratory therapist Byron Brimmer. "My dad and mother-in-law are living with me, but others are scattered all over the place, in Houston, and Austin, and Slidell."

Scattered was, in fact, the right word to describe what happened to many survivors of the Katrina flood. In the months after the disaster many people found more reasons to live elsewhere than to go back. EMT Carla Staxrud was living in California nine months after Katrina. Physician Steven Davidoff eventually landed in Texas. Marta Rozans and her two sons, Sam and Micky, stayed in Philadelphia for the entire school year. "Sometimes I'll be in the middle of class and I'll start thinking about what happened, and what might have happened," said Sam Rozans, who spoke to his classmates about the Katrina experience at a school assembly.

Nevertheless, most of Tulane's key staff stayed in the area. As the hospital rebuilt itself in the fall of 2005, it retained just about every single administrator.

As the human tragedy of Katrina began to be documented, many of HCA's people clung to individual anecdotes of people they had been able to help. For instance, there is the story of Davy, an eleven-year-old boy flown on a military helicopter to Lakeview Regional Medical Center in Covington on Thursday afternoon of that terrible week.[8] When his helicopter landed at Lakeview, Davy had no identification; in fact, months after Katrina, no one knew exactly where he had come from (it wasn't Tulane). Lakeview CEO Max Lauderdale carried Davy from the helicopter, because the boy said he couldn't walk. When the ER doctor examined Davy he discovered that both of his legs were very infected. "We eventually concluded that he had been walking around in the flood water and had scratched up his legs and they had gotten infected because of that," Lauderdale later said.

Lakeview physicians immediately put Davy on antibiotics, and they did minor surgery on him to drain his abscesses. But they still couldn't get the boy to talk, and of course they had no idea where his parents were, or even if his parents were alive.

The next day Lauderdale began breaking the ice with Davy. "When I came in, he was lying there in a hospital bed with his legs tied up in stirrups, having just eaten breakfast," the CEO said. "I asked him, 'Was breakfast good?' and he said it was, and I said, 'Do you want more?' and he said 'Yeah, I do!'" With TV out, the hospital staff tracked down a PlayStation game to keep Davy occupied. The hospital's social worker soon learned his full name, and learned that he had been separated from his parents after the flood. Through a series of phone calls to HCA's shelters in Lafayette, the company located Davy's father and aunt. On Sunday his aunt arrived at Lakeview by HCA-chartered helicopter. "When we took her up to see him he lit up like a Christmas tree, he was so happy," Lauderdale later said. On Tuesday his father picked him up.

Of course, there are as many stories about the personal impact of Hurricane Katrina as there were people who went through Hurricane Katrina. And, in terms of personal, financial, and emotional loss to peo-

---

[8] Davy's actual name was changed to protect patient confidentiality.

ple affiliated with HCA, you can't just talk about people who went through the Tulane airlift. There were, for instance, the other three-fourths of the Tulane Hospital employees, who eventually came home to assess the damage to their homes, neighborhoods, friends, and family members. There were the employees of HCA's other affected hospitals – most notably Garden Park Medical Center in Gulfport; Lakeview Regional Medical Center in Covington; DePaul-Tulane Behavioral Health Center in New Orleans; and Lakeside Hospital in Metairie. An account of these personal stories would fill many volumes.

The experience of being part of the airlift bonded the people who were at Tulane Hospital and affected them in a very profound way. An outsider, having seen footage and read articles about the horrors of the Hurricane Katrina flood, might think that the people who experienced it would be reluctant to discuss it afterward. In fact, just the opposite was true. More than eighty people were interviewed for this book. Everyone of them seemed eager, even anxious, to talk.

One theme that came up again and again in the interviews was a sincere gratitude toward Tulane's parent company. "I don't know what it cost to get us out of there, but what I do know is that our company paid a lot, and I am very grateful to them for doing so," said chief of nursing Danita Sullivan. "They told us that our safety was the most important thing, and they weren't lying. And I know that they now have a lot of employees who are completely dedicated to them because of this."

High praise for HCA didn't just come from its employees, either. Much of it came from doctors, who certainly had no obligation to praise the for-profit hospital company that owns one of the hospitals at which they practice. "Tulane and HCA in particular did a wonderful job," said Dr. Marta Rozans. "And for me to say that is really something, because I love to bash HCA. I mean, I'm a doctor, and that's what doctors do, is bash corporate. But they did an incredibly great job of getting patients out and getting us out, and of making sure we had food and medicine in between."

People who experienced the Tulane airlift also seemed proud of it, and, curiously, glad they had been part of it. "Assuming this had to happen, I wouldn't have wanted to have been anywhere else," said Dr. Lee Hamm. "And I suspect if you ask around you will find that many of the people who work for Tulane Hospital who weren't there now feel bad that they weren't there." In fact, in researching this book, this author would ask Tulane Hospital employees whether they were at the hospital during the flood. If they said no, they had a tendency to do it with a combination of regret and apology. "I wanted to work that weekend, but they told me not to come in," one Tulane security guard said.

"It kind of reminds me of the book I read about World War II called *Band of Brothers*," said HCA chief executive Jack Bovender. "Soldiers who have been through combat have a different kind of camaraderie than soldiers who haven't. I suspect that some of what happened at Tulane is similar to that."

Some people who went through the airlift took also away lessons that were bigger and broader than their relationship to their employer and their co-workers. Many of them came out of the experience with more self-confidence and more faith in God and humanity. Joe Lasky, the physician who waded through New Orleans after the flood and retrieved a National Guard truck from the Superdome, said the ordeal made him more optimistic about human nature. "I think I'm reassured a bit about what you can expect from a random stranger," he said. "I mean, there is something to be said about the fact that I walked over to the dome with no identification except for a stethoscope and was able to get help."

Cheryl Turano, who helped take care of fifty-eight "Superdome people" during the flood, and then went to the airport to help her mother Kim Ryan arrange Tulane's staging area, also said the experience affected her in many ways. "Little things don't matter to me anymore," she said. "What went wrong today doesn't matter anymore. What I drive doesn't matter to me anymore.

"And the way I feel about my city has changed. I used to hate New Orleans. Now I love the place. I can't explain why. But it's true."

Conclusion
Return of the Colors

E arly on Valentine's Day 2006 many members of the staff at Tulane Hospital, along with several employees from HCA's corporate office in Nashville, physicians, family members, friends, and members of the national and local media, migrated to the roof of the Saratoga Street Parking Garage. It was a clear, bright day, and positively nippy by New Orleans standards. They talked, smiled, and patted each other on the back. Some of them pointed at this corner of the garage, or that corner of the garage, as if to explain that this happened over here and that happened over there. And occasionally they searched the sky, looking for something.

About 8:30 they found what they were looking for: a small helicopter, painted red, white, and blue, growing on the horizon. After it made its way to the garage, it hovered, then slowly descended. As it landed, the backdraft made everyone hold their hats, or cover their eyes, or look away entirely. Some of the people in the crowd seemed sincerely surprised about the force of this backdraft. Others, who had learned quite a bit about helicopters a few months earlier, seemed unfazed by it.

When LifeNet's aircraft was on the deck, two crewmen jumped out and unloaded a stretcher. A dozen print and television photographers ran over to it, as if it contained the injured body of a celebrity. Then three members of Tulane's staff went up and carefully removed the only thing sitting on the stretcher: a large American flag, folded properly, with the stars showing. As Deputy Chief of Police Warren Breaux austerely carried the flag toward the elevator, practically everyone in the crowd applauded. Breaux and several other security people then took the flag back to the roof of the adjacent building – the one with the word "Tulane" and a big "H" on it – where they hung it in the precise location it had been a few months earlier.

About an hour later there was another ceremony down on LaSalle Street, one of the small roads adjacent to the main Tulane Hospital building. A large tent had been set up with bleachers adjacent to it and rows of chairs under it. The chairs were meant for local dignitaries and guests; the bleachers for the hundreds of doctors, nurses, and medical technicians on duty that day – the first day in six months Tulane Hospital was open to the general public. "I don't think I have ever seen so many people in lab coats squeezed into such a small area," CNN correspondent Sean Callebs wrote that day.

The enthusiasm of the audience made this second event more fun to attend than one might have predicted. While the crowd waited for the event to get started, there didn't seem to be any bored people, just happy ones. After a few minutes, the Tulane staff in the bleachers even began doing "the wave" to entertain the dignitaries.

Among the people who spoke that day was HCA president and chief operating officer Richard Bracken. "Tulane has been supporting Mardi Gras for 150 years, and we weren't going to let this one get by," Bracken said. Tulane chief executive Jim Montgomery made a few comments about the airlift, pointing out that the parts of the facility that were opening that day were the emergency room, the operating room, a laboratory, radiology, and the adult and pediatric intensive care unit – a total of sixty-three beds.

The crowd cheered just about everything said that day, and gave standing ovations several times. Once was when HCA's name was mentioned. Another was when New Orleans Mayor Ray Nagin was introduced. "It is time for the city's pity party to end today, and it will end with HCA Tulane," he said, getting a bit worked up. "Now, with Mardi Gras coming up and with the health care system so tight, who jumps up and supports us? Tulane/HCA to the rescue!"

Then came the obligatory ribbon cutting, followed by media tours of the facility, and then the finger foods. By noon the crowd had mostly dispersed. The staff of Tulane University Hospital and Clinic had work to do.

Afterword and Acknowledgements

When I started this project, I knew the story would be dramatic. I didn't foresee how complicated it would be.

Let me say a few things about the approach I used. First of all, like everyone else in America, I was glued to CNN and Fox News during the days after Hurricane Katrina. And, like most everyone else, I was frustrated by the coverage. I knew the reporters and producers were doing their best. But watching the story unfold, I found myself getting angry about aspects of the story that weren't being covered, questions that weren't being asked, and points that weren't being made. What emerged on television wasn't so much a story about what happened as it was snapshots of the misery, sometimes misinterpreted and then replayed over and over again. So that didn't help much.

After HCA asked me to research and write this book, I read every article I could find about the Tulane airlift in newspapers, popular magazines, and specialized medical journals. I reviewed several hours of CNN coverage of Katrina at the Vanderbilt Television News Archive. And, in May 2006, as I finished writing this book, I read the *Atlanta Journal-Constitution's* twenty-two-part series on the Tulane airlift.

It was a helpful exercise. But most of the articles and television segments I found contained mistakes. One newspaper reported that armed gangs attacked the hospital (not true). Another reported that the big American flag draped on the hospital had somehow been associated with 9/11 (a false rumor). A third reported that Tulane patients were still being evacuated on Saturday of that week (impossible).

In the name of artistic license many reporters also tried to retell the story of the Tulane airlift by focusing on a very small number of people to the exclusion of everyone else. Not only did this bruise a few egos, it also had a tendency to oversimplify the process and mislead the public about just how much went into its execution.

In fact, the most useful articles I found were first-person accounts of the event that appeared in various health care journals, such as *Congenital Cardiology Today* and *The New England Journal of Medicine*.

Eventually I concluded that newspaper articles, though helpful, could not be relied upon because reporters didn't have the time to get multiple points of view. And, more than any other event I've ever encountered, recounting the Katrina flood required multiple points of view.

Then I dove into the interview process. The book you hold in your hands is largely a product of those interviews. But, having said that, it should be pointed out that many of the people I interviewed for the book made mistakes as well. There were many disagreements about what, when, and why things happened. Some people had a tendency to talk about things they knew second-hand as if they knew them first-hand. One minute they would be talking about how hungry, tired, and worried they were through the whole ordeal (a subject on which they were an authority), and the next minute they would be blaming the mayor, or the governor, or the president for not allowing fuel trucks to get through (something on which they knew very little). As the interviewer, I had to differentiate between what people knew and what they thought they knew. Doing this often required follow-up interviews.

In the many situations where there were differences of opinion, I would go back to all involved people and re-ask the question. Then, if differences persisted, I would usually ask those people to communicate with one another and see if·they could figure out what happened. If that didn't work, I had to judge make an educated guess. The rule of thumb I used was to ask myself which of the people disagreeing here would be more likely to know the truth. In matters related to helicopters, for instance, I had a tendency to side with the pilots. When it came to medical questions, I went with physicians.

Re-creating this story through interviews was so difficult a process that I eventually came to two conclusions about human nature. One is that people have a tendency to get very confused when they are talking about something that took place over a five-day period during which they were hungry and tired the whole time. The other is that the Tulane airlift was one of those "bigger than life" events that changed the lives of just about everyone who went through it. I suspect events like that always take on mythical proportions as soon as they are over.

I say all this to emphasize that this book isn't perfect. Hurricane Katrina created such chaos and human misery in New Orleans that no one book can retell the story with complete accuracy. This book may contain honest mistakes. It may omit interesting anecdotes, or accounts that might shed important light, simply because I couldn't talk to everyone. I can, however, assure the reader that both HCA, which commissioned this work, and I, who researched and wrote it, did our very best, in the time that we had, to tell as complete a story as possible.

Finally, I want to say a special word of thanks to the following people:

To Dr. Marta Rozans, for editing help and for allowing me to use some of her photographs.

To Dr. Norm McSwain, who allowed me to use his photographs.

To Doctors Mike Kiernan, Bob Ascuitto, Nancy Ross-Ascuitto, and Steven Davidoff, for giving me copies of their personal journals kept during the ordeal.

To Sally and John Koch, who were nice enough to offer me a place to stay in Baton Rouge and to feed me when there wasn't a vacant hotel room within 200 miles.

And to everyone at Tulane and HCA who took time out of their busy schedules to talk to me and answer the many, many questions that came up during this process.

APPENDIX I

Jim Montgomery's Katrina Journal

Editor's note: Tulane CEO Jim Montgomery wrote this email and sent it to many of his friends and colleagues as soon as he had been airlifted out of Tulane. It has been edited.

In Bob Dylan's song *A Hard Rain's A-Gonna Fall*, the singer is asked, "Where have you been? What did you see? What did you hear? Who did you meet? And what'll you do now?" to which he answers with a collage of images that attempts to answer each question. In this crisis the images were moving so fast that I think it will take awhile to put it together. But here's an attempt to do so.

As of noon on Friday the 25th, the storm didn't seem like it would be much of an event, but by five p.m. things began to look different. We [the hospital staff] met as a group on Saturday to begin our routine preparations for a hurricane. Donna [my wife] left for her brother's home, and I went home to put things together there. I started to think, "What do I absolutely not want to lose in case the house would be swept away?" All I took were photos of the family and a few clothes.

When the storm hit on Sunday night, I reflected on the fact that God's natural world has an awesome power. From the small observation windows from our tallest floors, we observed awnings being blown off, a blinding rain and a general sense that if God is ever angry, we're going to lose big. Our first inspections revealed little damage: a few broken windows and some roof damage, but the building held up well. In fact, if you were in the inner core of the facility you only vaguely heard it. We even walked around late in the afternoon, since there was only limited flooding (no worse than a heavy thunderstorm). Overconfident, we even stated we had absorbed the best punch nature could throw and we seemed intact.

But at 1:30 a.m. on Tuesday morning began the biggest crisis and challenge of my life and in the history of Tulane and New Orleans. I was awakened by my COO, Kim Ryan, who told me the water in the boiler room had been rising a foot an hour since midnight. If it continued at that rate we had, at best, only another two to three hours before we would lose all power, since we already had been on emergency power since early Monday morning. We had seven ventilator patients whose lives would be in jeopardy, and we had to move fast to get them out. And we had no boat and no helicopter pad.

I called Acadian Ambulance, who I know well but who had no business connection to our hospital, and asked their immediate help. We had a parking deck connected to the hospital that we had evaluated as sturdy enough to support helicopter flight, but it had four light poles in the middle of it.

What happened during the next four hours was nothing short of a miracle. Our maintenance group got the light poles down. Acadian agreed to pick our patients up. We made arrangements with our other HCA hospitals to take them. Our staff and physicians got their patients ready. And, most importantly, the water rise began to slow to an inch per hour. A little after the sun came up, helicopters were on the roof and patients began to be transported.

Early on Tuesday morning we met with our key managers at the hospital. We prayed for support, comfort, and guidance for what we knew was going to be a difficult period. We talked about what we knew, and what we didn't know, which was considerable because we had no contact from FEMA or the mayor's office. We had no idea why water was rising and, from what limited facts we had, no one did. We had to assume that it would keep rising and we would lose power. Thus, no light, no air conditioning, no suction, no oxygen, no elevators, no phones – everything that is precious to good care.

We had to get out. So we hatched a plan, and I tried to stay out of the way. Physicians and nurses triaged patients; other people who work with me determined what vital supplies needed replenishing; and HCA worked frantically to coordinate a transportation effort to pick up patients and, eventually, our staff. "How many people?" HCA asked me. Good question. At least twelve hundred, which included 160 patients, employees and physicians and their families and seventy-six dogs and cats (which I didn't know about at the time).

Also on Tuesday, the looting began. We witnessed people – dozens of them – wading in front of the hospital with bag after bag of stuff. Bandits took over two hotels adjacent to us and forced out many of our employees' families who had been housed there. This sent them back into the hospital, creating further complications. That night our people on the roof evacuating patients heard gunshots, but they continued their work. The lawlessness and insurrection certainly was a distraction, but our Tulane Police were great, and they are very capable. Late in the day we ran out of fuel, so our generators shut down and the building began to get hot.

If you would like to know if we slept that night, try this experiment. Heat the bedroom up to about ninety or ninety-five degrees. First you're hot and then you sweat and get cold and then the cycle repeats.

At daybreak on Wednesday our patients were moved into a queue. I saw our staff, residents, and faculty move sick patients with a grace and dignity that was most impressive. This was our third day, and the stress on our people began to show. Everyone was asking when, where, and how were we going to get out. The city sewer system was obviously backing up, spilling out, and creating an acrid smell that over the next few days made it almost impossible to breathe. With no water pressure, none of us could bathe. But here's a general observation: If everyone smells the same, you really don't notice it; you just feel unclean.

On this day the Louisiana Wildlife and Fisheries Department showed up to help us move some patients we had inherited from the Superdome on Sunday night. These included over sixty medically needy people with chronic conditions. So by boat we sent them and their loved ones away. I met a woman whose most valuable possessions were her pillow and her radio. I promised her I would protect them. They are still in my office.

Then there appeared out of nowhere this guy, John Holland, who was sent in by HCA to be our Flight Coordinator - whatever that is. "The man" had arrived who would communicate with the birds in the air. This ended up being really important.

The Big Birds began to fly. Instead of one or two patients they could move up to four with some additional staff. They were a beautiful sight. By the end of the day we had moved all but about twenty patients, including two who weighed more than four hundred pounds and one artificial heart assist-device patient, which was the challenge of the week since the device itself weighed more than five hundred pounds. So imagine hauling this weight three to four floors down a dark stairwell at ninety-plus degrees. It was a young man's job and it was done. Let me tell you that the coordination from the patient's room to the staging area to the helipad into the helicopter was a work of art composed by many painters. It truly was a thing of beauty, and it touched everyone who was there.

By the end of day HCA had constructed an extraction plan for the remaining staff. The idea was that everyone take a helicopter to the airport, where they would then be taken by bus to Lafayette. Of course, this sounds good, but there were lots of details to work out. And we were very worried still about what the government might do.

On Thursday people were lining up and getting ready. By this time, we were basically were living on Strawberry Pop-Tarts, honey oat bars and tuna fish. Fortunately, I like all of these things, but I'm sure I lost ten pounds or so. Anyway, the line was formed and I personally counted seven hundred people (mainly our staff, physicians, and their families) and, to top it off, seventy-six dogs and cats. How are we going to deal with that? So we relegated them immediately to second-class citizenship to another line and prayed that we wouldn't have to put the pets to sleep if no one would haul them.

At first there were just a few small helicopters and we had some patients to move and it was slow. Moving through the line, people were calm with a few exceptions but overall they managed their plight well. Then a situation developed. A frantic director of critical care showed up by boat from Charity Hospital. Major problem. Charity was in a meltdown. He said that he had twenty-one critical care patients – many being hand-ventilated for two days – and he couldn't get any help from the state. "Can you help me?" he asked.

This was a tough question but it had only one answer. We would give them access to the small aircraft, which wasn't going to help us move our staff anyway. So that process began much to the chagrin of our non-professional staff and family. Our nurses and doctors performed masterfully, but the situation increased the crowd's intensity. By now it was midday, and it was moving slow. It didn't look good. Then several things happened.

A Chinook helicopter is big, with two rotors, and it carries about fifty or sixty people. It moves with a slow deliberate confidence hard to describe. On Thursday afternoon one showed up. We had questioned whether it could land, and we asked "the man, John." He said it could, but he said that nothing else could be on the pad when a Chinook landed because of turbulence. As it approached, cheers broke out from below. So for a few hours we made real progress. But then it stopped.

What happened? I didn't know. I called my daughter Megan, and she seemed elated. "You're back," she said. "What?" I asked. She told me that Governor Blanco had just announced that Tulane had totally been evacuated. But she was about four hundred people short in her analysis. So we now had a new problem: They think we're not here.

I called the Louisiana National Guard. And along came a real coincidence. Guess who answered? A young man named Brad Smith, who had just been at Tulane a day earlier, because his daughter had been one of our patients. He had gotten a ride back and was now flying sorties into New Orleans. He quickly got ahold of the Office of Emergency Preparedness and let them know we still needed help. So we figured we might get out Friday.

People were remarkably calm when we told them they'd be there another day. They just sat down and began to prepare to go to bed.

We left the hospital and remained in the parking deck. We did this for three reasons. One, it was cooler. Two, there would be less confusion in the morning. And, three, it was safer since there was less territory for our Tulane Police to patrol. I know the media has played up the anarchy, and no doubt there was some concern, but I always thought we were safe.

Thursday night was interesting. Imagine trying to fall asleep on your concrete driveway without a pad or pillow. It's kind of tough. Then, throw in an unexpected helicopter landing at one a.m. The wind is a little dicey. The bird dropped off fifty percent of the Marines in New Orleans: one guy [Sergeant Kraft] who needed to go to Charity. So we took him over.

The next event for the evening took place at four a.m. when we were treated to a massive explosion at a warehouse on the river several miles away. I happened to be looking directly at it at the time. It must have reached a thousand feet in the air. Then, by the end of the evening, we began actually to get cold.

The end was pretty anti-climatic. At eight a.m. on Friday, Chinooks began showing up taking sixty people at a time. I wonder if our pilot friend in the guard had anything to do with it, but I don't know if I'll ever know. So in a matter of two and a half hours, everyone was gone except our police and the last remnants of management. Then, after attempts to arrange coordination with Charity to use the helipad, we left for home sweet home.

I talked to the chairman of the board of HCA upon returning and told him it was the worst and most difficult challenge I have ever been personally involved with. But at the same time, I told him that I don't think that I've ever felt as great a sense of accomplishment from anything I've been involved with. Our staff performed like clockwork, and it was a beautiful thing to observe. And our success was simply measured by the fact that we didn't lose a patient during this trying time.

APPENDIX II

Some of the emails received by Jack Bovender in the weeks after Katrina

Two years ago I resigned from the New Orleans Police Department to take a job with Tulane, and I was one of the eighteen police officers there during Hurricane Katrina. I, along with my family, want to take this time to thank you for your commitment to getting us out of the most dangerous conditions I have ever experienced. I will never be able to thank you enough for saving so many lives, including mine. Your staff – all of those tireless souls who worked around the clock – are the best I have ever seen, and it was an honor to serve and protect them. I would volunteer to go back with that team under any circumstances.

Officer Penny Young

I am proud to be a staff member at an HCA hospital (Southwest Medical Center in Lafayette, Louisiana). During the recent hurricane HCA showed it really cares for its employees and their families. They provided not only a safe evacuation of Tulane Medical Center, but also provided their evacuating employees and their families with a place to shower, get free clothing, food, medical treatment, and a place to stay. These people were very grateful for all the help they received. It is a pleasure to see a large company like HCA taking care of its employees. I am proud of HCA, especially the staff and doctors at Southwest Medical Center who worked well into the early morning hours to ensure that the evacuating employees got the help they needed. Thank you for placing people before profit.

Bryan G. Frentz, MD

I was proud and grateful to see HCA going strong to assist everyone affected by Hurricane Katrina. It was humanitarian. With the updates from Jack Bovender and other emails that were sent out to us, I shared the information with others and my family. And thank you for establishing the HCA Hope Fund.

Suzie Adkins
Accountant, St Joseph's Hospital
Parkersburg, West Virginia

I am a staff nurse in the Tulane emergency room. Thank you, HCA, for all your efforts in the Tulane evacuation. Because you were there for me and my family, I will be there when Tulane reopens. Words cannot convey the depth of my gratitude.

God bless,
Michael R. Condatore

Until this very moment I never understood the magnitude of concern that HCA has for people in general. I cannot commend you enough for your thoughtfulness and your help to those less fortunate than we. I am proud to say that my husband is affiliated with such a wonderful group of people. To all of you: much gratitude and many blessings of thanks.

Tracey Dickerson-Clark
[Wife of Robert Clark, St. Petersburg General Hospital]

Thanks for your magnificent performance at Tulane Hospital. Your efforts to sustain, protect, and evacuate patients were outstanding. Jim Montgomery and Jeff Tully were untiring in their exertions. Jim actually herded us onto helicopters as we departed on September 2, and Jeff never slept while interacting with the employees and medical staff. I hope that the corporation and those employees that made this a successful effort get the credit deserved. They stood tall in our hour of need.

Robert N. Jones, Emeritus Professor
Tulane School of Medicine

I was one of the Tulane physicians helicoptered out during the Katrina crisis. Words cannot express my gratitude to HCA for the magnificent way the evacuation was planned and executed. Every step was foreseen, even to providing Benadryl to people prone to airsickness. It figures that Jim Montgomery would be in the last group out. He, among others, was a source of strength and inspiration to all of us. After the helicopter ride to the New Orleans airport, we found medical professionals of competing hospitals who were basically abandoned at the airport. The HCA personnel on site took them onto the buses and transported them to safety. One doctor in particular said he would have died if not for HCA. HCA is a first-rate company that showed real class in the way that they took care of their employees and staff.

Peter R. Kastl

I just wanted to say that in 25 years of being in healthcare, never have I been so proud to be affiliated with an employer as I am at this moment. To see the massive effort by HCA and all of our employees in the wake of Hurricane Katrina was truly heartwarming. The staff pulled together like nothing I have ever seen before. Whatever management asked of us, we rose to the occasion. I am truly proud to call myself an employee of HCA. Thank you for all you have done for the victims of this terrible disaster and for your employees.

Monique Moreland
Southwest Medical Center
Lafayette, Louisiana

Thank you, HCA, for all you have done. My wife [Barbara] and I are medical technologists at Lakeside Hospital in Metairie. We are so proud of how HCA handled its employees after Katrina and Rita. To know that a paycheck was coming in while we were unable to work was a comfort when our hearts were hurting so much. So many of our friends and coworkers have lost so much. Some have stayed, but many have moved out of the state. We will miss them. When our hospital opened again on September 29th, we never knew we would be so happy to go back to work. I have told many people that I work for a great organization. Thank you again for the much needed help you supplied not only to my family but to all those in need and also to the generous donations you made.

Tom Rosselot

I would like to thank you for all you have done throughout the entire Hurricane Katrina ordeal – sending us food and supplies, rescuing us when the government had abandoned us, and giving us financial support when we had to wait to get through to FEMA and the Red Cross. Thankfully and gratefully you have stood by the side of some of your most faithful employees as they tirelessly attended to patients in the days after Hurricane Katrina. I know that this disaster is creating a hardship on the company, but I am grateful that you have stood by us. I hope I can return to Tulane soon to work with the doctors, nurses, technicians, and others that put patient care and comfort above all odds.

Melody Sanchez

I am an employee of Tulane Hospital who was working as an RN coordinator in the transfer center when Hurricane Katrina hit New Orleans. Nothing prepared us for what happened, but HCA's immediate response to the needs of its employees and its continued support will never be forgotten. The administration of Tulane and HCA deserves and has my eternal gratitude and loyalty.

God bless,
Mary (Beth) Shipley

I am a former employee of Tulane Hospital. My job was lost due to Hurricane Katrina, after eight wonderful years in the information systems department. Thank you for the continuation of paychecks and benefits until December 31. As if that blessing wasn't enough, you also gave us a wonderful severance package, and offered assistance in obtaining other HCA positions throughout the country. I'm proud to say I was an employee of HCA and pray that one day I may be a part of your team again. However, if not, you will always have my deepest respect and gratitude. May God continue to bless this great institution.

Karen J. Smith
Grand Prairie, Texas

I am a registered nurse employed by Tulane Hospital in New Orleans, and I was working at Tulane during Hurricane Katrina. I wanted to thank you for evacuating our patients and our staff to safety. Additionally, HCA went above and beyond to ensure that we received paychecks. I was able to utilize All About Staffing, which helped me secure a travel position in the emergency room of West Florida Hospital in Pensacola, Florida. Everyone I've dealt with at HCA, All About Staffing, and West Florida Hospital has been wonderful. I am proud to continue my employment with HCA.

Ron Stein

I want to thank you for the buses that came from our sister hospital (Southwest Medical Center) in Lafayette. Our patients received food, medicine, and treatment. I am now safe at my mother's house in Ruston, Louisiana, but am willing to go back in to help others as soon as we are allowed. If I did not work for a company like HCA, I would still be stranded. There really are no words to tell you how grateful we are.

Ann Wilder
DePaul-Tulane Behavioral Health Center,

I was the clinical manager for the transplant unit at Tulane. I wanted to thank you for continuing our pay and benefits through the end of the year. Your kindness has allowed us to rebuild our home and kept our daughter in college, and you made a horrible experience tolerable. You will never know how many people your decision touched. I can never repay your kindness.

Kim Wilkerson

My daughter, Claire, was a nurse at Tulane Hospital during Hurricane Katrina and spent four days there until she was rescued by HCA. I cannot express the gratitude we have for your commitment to your employee's safety and well-being. She performed her job under very difficult circumstances, and you cared enough to bring her home to us in one piece. We are so thankful that you took care of her and made sure she was OK until we picked her up in Lafayette that Thursday night. We were frantic about her getting out, given the unsafe environment she was in. We cannot thank you enough for getting her out and continuing to touch base with her as she decides where she will go next. HCA deserves recognition for handling the evacuation of their own, much better than FEMA, the state, or anyone else involved could have done. You certainly rose to the occasion and did what was right - if only that could have been done for many others who weren't so blessed. You will always have our gratitude for taking care of our daughter.

Harold and Lyle Leleux
Rayne, Louisiana

Index